Black
Witch

Black Witch

Steve Scott

authorHOUSE®

AuthorHouse™
1663 Liberty Drive
Bloomington, IN 47403
www.authorhouse.com
Phone: 1-800-839-8640

www. steveelofscott.com
Cover Design by Rebel Digital

Published by AuthorHouse 01/27/2015

ISBN: 978-1-4918-7019-8 (sc)
ISBN: 978-1-4918-7020-4 (hc)
ISBN: 978-1-4918-7021-1 (e)

Library of Congress Control Number: 2014904399

Print information available on the last page.

This book is printed on acid-free paper.

Dedication

I would like to dedicate this book to the three women who made this book happen. One, my daughter Tasha who inspired it all, who first tested and then saved my sanity. Becky, who loved and cared for me during my darkest times. And the Strawberry Blonde Enigma, Sherry, Natasha's mother, who showed me that love is not ephemeral. Love is eternal and certainly it is redeemable.

The events of this book are now engrained in the Granite of history. As you will learn in this book, the spirit of my Natasha lives still, in the heart of her mother and mine. She lives with us always.

Author's note

The events of this book are real, if not entirely true. Truth is something that is verifiable by some sort of consensus. The events of this book are real. They happened fifteen years ago and more. I was fifty then, now I'm staring down the path of Medicare. What happened in those days was heightened and probably distorted by stress and alcohol, but they were real all the same. So, Walter Cronkite was the last truth I'm sure of, the dream I had three nights ago was real.

"Our minds are the fitful flashes of an eternal light" -- Spinoza

Beware. If you don't believe that spirits are real, leave now. If you don't think that there is a killer buried beneath the cortex of your brain under layers of generations, you don't belong here. If you don't believe that next to that killer, buried a little less deep, is a force that can test your sanity, possess your heart and shade your days, drop this book back where you found it and go get some soup for your soul. If you view tragedy as a twenty point drop in the NASDAQ, I have nothing to say to you. If you enter here, you will find that spirits do exist. You will find that sometimes you have power over them and sometimes they have power over you. You will have to decide on your own if God exists. He does exist here, in this book, though you may not recognize him. If you think that it is important to feel good all the time and that there is no value in feeling bad sometimes, then I suggest the comic book section. If you want to feel what it's like to have something grip your heart like a vice and have control over you, step inside. If you give credence to words like "depression" and not words like "demon," please leave now. If you don't like me, so what? I probably don't like you either. In any case, I think it is better if most of you leave now. On days like this, I am better left alone.

Chapter I

IN THE LIGHT OF BETTER DAYS

"God not only plays dice, he throws them where
they can't be seen." Stephen Hawking

D o you like words? I do. Words are like a mistress. She can
enchant you, enrage you, seduce you. Make you feel like a
man, or leave you wanting in the morning. It goes without
saying that she will deceive you. I guess the word that best described me
during the days of the Black Witch is "anchorite;" a hermit, a recluse
who has withdrawn from the world for religious reasons without joining
an order.

This day, I sat high on a ridge overlooking a wide open vista
pondering the words "anchorite" and "religion" and I laughed at the
irony. In front of me, stretching to the horizon, was an immensity of
possibilities. Behind me the same. The Ray Mountains in front of me
were an unending wave of blue, stretched horizon to horizon. That wave
was capped with the dazzling white foam of a snowy crown. Between
those mountains and me was the fertile valley of anything possible.
Behind me, the rocky crag of a barren peak was like the sight on a
rifle. It aimed at a layering of ridges that dropped in shelves all the way
down to the Yukon River. The great river stretched away forever. My
head was filled with the beauty of it all. It had not always been this way.
But then, I had spent the better part of the last three years on a search
for something of value within me. That search had been conducted on
a field strewn with dead people and the often infertile ideas of others.

You can however, also often find wisdom and value in the eternal spirits of those dead people. One of those dead people had offered up some solace and some balm. He had been dead for three hundred years, nearly four hundred. The spirit of a dead man now resided comfortably in my head. "For if salvation were ready to hand and could be discovered without great toil, how could it be that it is almost universally neglected? All things excellent are as difficult as they are rare."

Three years after misery had poured over me like fast hardening cement, I found myself now, on a mission of love. I was trying to capture what was left to me in my remaining days. I was on a mission to save what had once been mine. I was on a mission to regain a friendship that was so important to me. And I was on a mission to find out if any of it was possible. What was key though, was the fact that I was on a mission. That was more important than the success of the mission. I was alive and kicking once again.

The mission was to drive across a couple hundred miles of Alaskan wilderness in the springtime on snow machines with some friends and rescue an airplane that I had crashed in the river valley that lay between the ridge where I now sat and those far away Ray Mountains. And though my planning may have been half-assed, that was just part of my nature. The effort I was about to expend to get that airplane would be the best I had to offer. And as always, I was blessed with good luck and good companionship. I was laying it all out and would accept the result that I achieved. I was trying again. I was me again, and for whatever that was worth, I was now trying to accomplish something that was very important to me. I was trying to resurrect an airplane and the long dormant man who had flown that airplane. Sidetracked for almost fifteen years by life in America, I was in search of whatever value lay inside me.

I had wondered lately about what constitutes value. What makes a person as unique as a snowflake? A person's character. A person's character is nothing more than the sum total of his experiences, forged and tempered by the spirit that resides within, a soul if you will. I have come to believe that a person's soul is the single thing that is his alone. Whatever this soul thing is, this spirit thing, it does exist and it is the defining uniqueness that separates all human beings.

I have a friend, Jody, who is an artist with a welder and a torch. On a recent visit to his house, he showed me a piece of art he had constructed from common workshop items. Bolts, bearings, nuts and a sheet of tin. A fragment from his mind, a street scene from a rainy Seattle day of years ago had lain in his memory like a child in a coma for twenty years. One day he had just begun. He rescued that lonely child of his memory and breathed life into that mental synapse. That charged particle from his brain became an almost animate, three-dimensional figure of substance…but more than that.

The scene is a lonely back alley entrance to a bar. It is complete with streetlamp, street signs, parking meter, two garbage cans and a mailbox. An old motorcycle is parked in the rain. There is no physical evidence of rain, but you know it's raining, just as you know that James Dean parked that motorcycle and he is inside a bar nearby, drinking.

The ability to imbue a sense of time, place and actual life into an inanimate object, is in my way of thinking, Jody's spirit transcending his physical body and inhabiting that piece of art. It is said that the Navaho have a similar belief. It is said that those people of visions believe that if a person puts himself entirely into his work, does the best he can, that with skill and patience, his soul will inhabit a thing as arcane as a hand-woven basket or as mundane as a Seattle street scene on a rainy day. I can imagine a time two hundred years from now when Jody's art resides in a place of prominence on a mantel somewhere. Jody's spirit will live as long as that piece of art exists. Jody's ghost will be sitting at that bar waiting for the rain to stop so he can remount that motorcycle and ride off into eternity.

I believe that spirits live in the creations of those who are gone. I believe, that while a person inhabits this physical, this real world, that person's spirit is like a dipped, poised pen or a wet brush. A person's spirit has the power to impose its presence on other things and other people, and therefore exist forever. I think a person's character has been painted by the spirits of many dead men and varnished by its experience. A person's spirit, his soul, inspired by the sum of that person's character is the Dynamic Creative Force, a fragment of God. A person's character is the reservoir of whatever talent that it is endowed with by that great, unknown force. A person's divine task is to use the media best suited to his talent. Once the media for a person's spirit to thrive in is learned or revealed, it is then up to the content of a person's character to hone and shape that spirit, set it free and let it fly. Only then can that person make a unique contribution to the world. Only then will that person's spirit be released to join others of its kind in that place commonly referred to as heaven.

As I sat high on a ridge in a place of such spectacular beauty, the awe that heaven must inspire was easily summoned on this day. Heaven? God? There was a point in my life that I never believed. But then I came to understand it really wasn't a matter of disbelieving or believing. It was only a matter of perception. And there are many, many perceptions. I've only had time to look at a few. I give you one man's perception. In the novel *Solaris* by Stansilaw Lem, you find two scientists on a faraway planet. The sanity and will of each has just been tested. The conclusion one of them arrived at?

God is an evolving being, not a static, pre-formed one. In Abraham's time, God was a baby, the cosmos, his crib. He demanded sacrifices and total submission, because like all babies, the only universe was his own elemental needs. As history unfolded, so grew our God. And like us mortals, trapped in our finite, insignificant lives, God is trapped in the role of the Omniscient One, but his life is infinite. And he is learning as he goes. Now, in our lifetime? Maybe he is stumbling through his adolescence, his power outweighing his knowledge, his ambition outweighing his power. He's inherited this eternity thing, and a truth which is immutable. Both of these cosmic treasures he hoped to use as a vehicle to understand his power and then as a means to imprint these same truths into infants whose welfare he has been given care of. But all He has done is set free a bacteria which infects a generation of self-serving ova over which he has a limited control. A Frankenstein top set spinning. Now as he sees his top spinning away, he's upset. He has paternal control of these infants born of His bacteria. Infants of infinite potential. These infants are the seed of his truths, but the infants will not be guided by these same immutable truths. Now we have an Angry God. So just what is this heaven thing that we are so intent on finding? A utopia run by a teenager? But of course this version of God is only the perception of a fictional character. There are many, many other perceptions.

I'm an average guy of average intelligence. I have had my sanity and will tested. I have come to some conclusions. I have discovered that God does exist. God endowed the soul that each of us possess with the bacterium of divine infinity. I have discovered that the mind imperfect computer that is littered with seeds and viruses. God did not plant those seeds in your mind. Those seeds were planted and sown there by genetics. God did not plant those viruses in there. Those viruses were planted there by another force or forces. And those forces must be the antithesis of God. Maybe one of the many antitheses of God. I don't believe in the devil. And I am only on a face-to-face basis with one of those viruses. I call that virus the Black Witch. God took a survey of the viruses and seeds each of us possess and then he planted a single thing into us: our soul. And with that soul, we must map out our journey and we must do the best we can with what we have in the face of all these viruses and seeds. God matches his souls with their travails and he watches... and maybe he learns.

I believe that God planted a single spark of divinity in each of us. That spark is there to deal with all the seeds and viruses, but more than that. That spark is there to allow each individual a small measure of impact. And that small impact is our tether to the mind of God and to his infinity. God knows this all ahead of time of course and there you have the great mystery. God knows of our impact, expects it, demands it but is somehow influenced by it. In the way of great actors, we bring life to the script of God through our small performances.

The mind is an intricate and incredibly complex...*thing*. It has evolved over millennia. During that time, I believe that the blight of the ages has been stamped into it. These blight-like viruses remain buried in the sterile ground of our intelligence. When stress, crises and melancholia rain down misery on our lives, those viruses are given nourishment. This virulence springs into life, real life, not imagined. Centuries-old viruses, not genetic disorders, but viruses passed on *by* genetics are then given free rein in the venue of modern day life, to raise havoc. And they use tools that we don't understand, nor have any rational device with which to deal. Enter the soul.

God has provided the antidote for all the viruses. We call that antidote the "soul." The genetic psychic-seeds are another matter. The viruses, when they bloom, immediately become aware of these psychic-seeds and use them to advantage. Who prevails in the battle that ensues is either the virus or the soul. The containment vessel that houses both the soul and the virus never wins. For him the battle never ends, and he eventually dies. What follows is the story of one such battle.

I was unaware of the fact at the time, but as I sat high on the ridge that day, my mind was like the still heated brain of a just recovered malaria victim. It was living with the residue of that fever, the delusions. But the fever was down and the mind was starting to make sense again. My recent battle had changed me somehow, back towards that recognizable person of twenty years ago. What scars that battle had left on me would be known in the days to come. So, armed with a brain that was returning to normal and with a body that I had toned up somewhat, I was blasting off on a journey of undetermined length into the heart of a wilderness as complete as any I ever hoped to explore.

Unknown to me at the time, while my companions took care of most of the decisions, I let the pure air and vivid images of perfection in this wilderness do what it would to enhance the process of healing still going on in my head. My brain was being released to relive those black days, put them to rest and come to some conclusions. My friends, some old, some recent, would write the whole process off to my drifty nature and let me tag along. I touched the starter, pulled on my helmet and followed in the wake of a blue exhaust mist and headed down into the valley toward the far away mountains of blue. I was about to take out my scalpel and go looking for that Black Witch in the days that followed. Days of a boreal beauty, breathtaking in their stark purity as well as soul-cleansing in nature's arena of pure air and physical exertion. And I thought about those dark days.

My battle began long before I ever recognized it. I suppose it began when the woman I had lived with for five years left me. She took her son, whom I had claimed as my own, with her. She took our daughter with her too. She moved two thousand miles away and left me alone.

It wasn't until much later that I knew that there was even a battle going on. It was later still that I was able to summon any defenses. Those defenses became evident only when I was able to review the battle from the immaculate edifice of God's back porch. On a snow machine ride on a picture-perfect day, one given to me by God, I was able to begin to understand the nature of the battle and the nature of my defenses. For those of you who do not know, there is a salve for the soul for each of us. My salve is the unfettered world of wide-open vistas. Backwoods Alaska.

Due to circumstances beyond my control, I was being forced by the United States government to plan and execute a snow machine ride across two weeks of time and a couple hundred miles of Alaskan ness. The purpose of this snow machine ride was to rescue an airplane that I had crashed there many years ago. When I was about two days into that journey, a strange thing happened. The hassles of everyday life dropped from my life like snow falling from a tree when you shake it. My days were filled with physical activity and my nights with good companionship. My senses were on a joyride of pure air and spectacular scenery. My mind opened up and unrefined, unblemished thoughts started pouring out like water through the spillway of a great dam. I became aware for the first time in many years. And other thoughts that had been penned up in the reservoir behind the dam of dead-end thinking were brought to the table of inquisition and dissected there. Most of the decisions made pertinent to the success of my airplane rescue were made by other people. I was surrounded by the competence and good company of some precious friends and left alone to my own thoughts.

It turned out that God was real and so were a few friends. In the pure cold air of backwoods Alaska, I was first able to start to make sense of the many words I had read over the years. Everybody, it seems, has an idea of what spirituality is, but no one has been really able to nail it down. That's because you can't. It is not supposed to happen.

And if you don't believe in God, how can you believe in nature? I was sitting on my snow machine looking out over a wilderness so pure that these thoughts actually popped into my head, "God and nature." But the demands of the trail interrupted all of that. We had twenty more miles to go and were on a timetable. So I touched the starter, my iron dog growled into life and I set off towards those blue and white mountains. We were going to slice our way through this beautiful vision until we came upon that place where my airplane lay buried beneath it. Along the way I intended to let my mind wander. I was determined to make some sense out of the roadblocks that prevented pure reason from wedding with spirituality. I was a hillbilly set out to have a few beers and a friendly chat with Moses, Robert Pirsig, Albert Camus, Spinoza....

Aside with a hillbilly

My background, heritage and inclination has always demanded that I resolve any issue I encounter with the mediation of common sense. If I am unable to do that, I will resort to a friend's advice.

There is no common sense to the death of your little girl. Friends advice amounts to well-meaning platitudes and a card from Hallmark. Most are simply helpless in the inherent ignorance of something that is by nature, implacable. When I was faced with a situation that was incomprehensible and unchangeable, I retreated to books. So, I started looking for books that dealt with death, religion, philosophy, etc. I found a book that stirred something in me as the words in its pages flowed through me. I found a voice that spoke to me from the armies of words that had marched before me over the years.

The voice that spoke to me belonged to Howard Bahr. He writes about the Civil War. There is a philosophy that resounds in one of his books, *The Black Flower*. That philosophy is that every man lives in the exact center of a personal universe bound by laws that apply to him alone. Every person lives in a universe created by manifestations generated by his God. Maybe his God is the Universal God of Christianity, maybe not. Regardless, His universe is as unique as an individual snowflake. There are as many universes as souls that inhabit the earth, or at least that is how it feels. Each soul is beholden to the tenets that form the truths of his particular universe. But everybody is caught up in the maelstrom of daily life.

It is interesting how in this book the soldiers of either side hold no particular animosity toward the other side. Mostly, they like each other. But their universes have been thrown violently together. As soon as a battle begins, they start killing each other. Our reality, like theirs, is simply the collision of our universe with those with whom we come into contact. Each universe contains its own set of values, its own rules. Within the universe of the main protagonist of the book was a simple and profound worship of the Lord. For that man, there was a way out of his mess.

That's kind of how my life had been for some time. I had been caught up in a maelstrom of events, but the twist was that most of the events were of my own making. But then I had lost control of those events. I began to feel like I was being swept along by events beyond my control. But I was lacking in that profound worship of the Lord, or any Lord.

It seems that we all get launched into life on our own when we leave home to find our place in the world. At this point in time we are armed with our common sense, whatever level of education we have reached, values instilled in us by our parents, our friends and teachers, the church and the experiences that have shaped our daily lives so far. And from the very beginning, the world is like a gigantic cement mixer. We are a single pebble in the mix and we are tossed violently around by the many forces in this great mixer of life. The mix of which we are a part, is in a perpetual state of dynamic change. Then it begins. You first experience the reality of things that go against your personal value system. Armed with preconceptions and ideals, we set forth and come under an immediate assault. The process of living through this can change us beyond recognition.

Many people remain in the relative security of places and people they have always known. Some do not. Some people find themselves at a time and place when the giant cement mixer of life reaches such a level of chaos, that their sanity is tested. Say at the height of a battle, the Tet offensive, The Chosin Reservoir, Iwo Jima, The Argonne Wood, Antietam, Valley Forge. People who participated in those great events are forced to step out of their personal universe, that universe that has nurtured them up to that pivotal point. Suddenly, they are forced to step out of the person who they are, the universe they know. In a split second of time, they find themselves in a maelstrom of events controlled by others, or maybe by no one. When you abandon who you are, you become a creation of the forces that control events and exist only within the rules of this new, unknown, chaotic storm, losing your personal universe in the process. All the values of your personal universe are furtive dust fragments, blown away by the winds of this new storm. You must survive; it is the imperative of nature. You must survive. Your personal value system is like a tentative barricade as you face the challenges of the reality of this great event. We all do it. Some of us face more dramatic reality checks than do others. For those esoteric few who are forced to face the monster within, become the monster within, they are changed and changed forever. The rest of us are left to wonder about them, mock them, or simply dismiss them. But for the vagaries of certain events, those people could be us. That knowledge is vital. For those men who faced the absolute surreal chaos of the heat of battle, it is my belief that the paramount stress pouring into their brain rained down nourishment on the seeds of their heritage. The Viking, Hun, or Warrior who has lain there dormant his entire life. The barbarian who is capable of rape and murder is released and takes control of the situation while the normal man is left to watch. I had never seen that Hun or that Viking. I have never reached that paramount point of stress. But I had worked my way down into the inner portion of the brain, maybe a layer or two away from that Viking, and I've glimpsed them. By rooting around in there, just short of that Viking, I believe that you don't let loose any saviors, but only demons. But those demons will try to save you. Those demons are the residue of evil, or the fighting of evil, from another age.

If you know any Vietnam veterans, or veterans of any American war, who have participated in close combat, you will find they are different. They are changed by it and either won't talk about it, or don't have the words to express that difference. They can only really talk about those times to another who has experienced the same bitter reality. I can't speak for them, but as a writer and observer I have to try to give my spin on it. I think it has to do with what happens when you learn absolutely of what you are capable. Chemicals such as adrenalin and others (Since World War I, the militaries of the major powers have provided their soldiers with substances that are not very different, chemically, from methamphetamine, when those soldiers enter into combat situations.) provide these soldiers with the means to amplify that ancient human that lies at the core of all people. Stress is the trigger that releases that man. Later, after the battle, those soldiers are left to relive that experience and there are no words to describe it. But they know, as do their comrades and no one else. That information is vital. All of us could be exposed to something that could test our sanity. Over the years people have told me how they would react given this or that situation. Bullshit! No one knows and that's why you have Vietnam vets that look at you blankly and just shake their head. Why? Because there are situations in which you find yourself, that drives you away from civilization and you become that thing in the jungle that screams from beyond the trees.

It's a tragedy for this country that Mr. Bush and Mr. Obama, among others, were never subjected to that experience. It's too bad that their children won't be asked to live that experience, then relive it in dreams. Maybe then things could be different in this country.

Coming to terms with this idea, I was able to begin to form my own ideas about religion. I sifted through ideas and thoughts I had had over the years and pounced on things that seemed to make sense, or at least empower me to get through the day. I came to believe that organized religions and politics are just consensus-forming organizations created to try to bond many same-thinking individuals into common blocks and impose their views on a given portion of the population. The shrinking of the world and the resulting clash of these bound up collusions of universes has weakened those organized bonds. In any case, the ideas of right and wrong propagated by these organizations are under siege. The ultimate truths are known only to the deities. People on the perimeter, those blessed with keen insight and boundless faith, are given a glance at those deities. Assimilation of any great cosmic truths by the masses is impossible by the nature of the inadequacy of purely intellectual thought to penetrate those truths. I believe even those of genius level are but highlighted points of light in a universe of lights. The wisdom of God is so great that we are a single 0 or 1 in the great binary program that is God's wisdom. At some point the unknown things, the spirituality of the cosmos, can be intellectually perceived only by God, and glimpsed at by the very few out there on the perimeter, those highlighted lights, so-called geniuses. So for simple people like me, you are bound by your faith, or you are captive of your intellect, left to make the ultimate cosmic wager.

Most of us folks are left to choose one of the religious conventions, normally a branch of Christianity that works best for us. Charlatans and those whose universes possess no salvation are then free to feed upon us folks. If you let them. The truths or values exist only in your individual universe. Be true to those values and you are true to your soul. The soul is the fiber of your spirituality. Defend yourself against charlatans and heathens and when the truth is finally revealed to you (or not), you simply have to exist with the consequences. To say there is a universal truth and expend all our energies searching for it is to open your intelligence to manipulation. Simply let your values exude from your soul, be true to those values and let paradise materialize as it will, around you. Avoid those who try to supplant values that are contrary to your soul. Walt Whitman said it best. "Dismiss whatever insults your soul."

This kind of thinking seems to be a poor way to spend a good vacation. In my case it was necessary. My life had been a wreck for some time and I had to get to the root of it. And I had stumbled on the perfect place for just this type of thinking. My two week adventure into the back country of Alaska was spent in an environment so unlike present day America that all reference was soon washed from my senses. Once that barricade had been removed, my thoughts no longer had to be formed in the context of our present civilization. This trip, though interrupted on one or two occasions by intrusions of modern day America, for the most part was free of civilization, that multifaceted octopus of demands and diversion. I was able to turn my focus within and study the contagion of self that infects modern life. And in the process search for the vaccine that might, if not eradicate that contagion, at least smother it for a time.

I had in the last couple of years begun to read the Bible on a daily basis. I had also taken a cursory tour through some of the more renowned philosophies of the ages. I had been in search of a logical way out of the black cloud that so darkened my days. Whenever something made sense to me, I would take a good look at it. I was attempting to dissect the idea of spirituality with the razorblade of logic and somehow wed the two. I never considered that the razorblade of logic might have been dulled by bias or politics. Nor did I consider that you cannot carve into something that inhabits an alien dimension with the razorblade of reality. But I was methodical in my pursuit and persevered.

The idea of virtue is as divergent as the different philosophies and religions that have existed since man first gained insight. I think all these different bodies of thought are really just telling you to be true to yourself, your conscience, don't sin. Baruch Spinoza lived in the middle part of the seventeenth century. He studied the Bible, the Talmud and several ancient philosophers. He was, what I reverently refer to, as a freak. In 1656 he was telling his friends that, and here I quote from the book *The Story of Philosophy* by Will Durant. "God might have a body--the world of matter; that angels might be hallucinations; that the soul might be merely life; and that the Old Testament said nothing of immortality." The fact that Spinoza flew in the face of his Jewish religion caught my sense of the irreverent. So I took a good look at Spinoza and found a friend and ally. Spinoza says, "Before all things, a means must be devised for improving and clarifying the intellect." Paraphrased by Durant, "We must distinguish carefully the various forms of knowledge and trust only the best."

That went right to the heart of the soul thing. You do this and you are being virtuous or spiritual. The duty to adhere to the demands of your soul is what makes each person special; it's what defines spirituality.

Years ago, I read a book by a guy named Robert Pirsig. In it, *Zen and the Art of Motorcycle Maintenance,* he makes the contention that the Bible is simply a guidebook to accomplish this. All the events in the Bible may very well have happened. What happened for certain, is that all the events in the Bible were perceived to have happened, or metaphorically, were perceived to have happened to the people who wrote them down. Whether this was a matter of hard reality, immaculate visions or mass hypnosis is inconsequential. This particular guidebook lays down its Ten Commandments which are rules that are good social standards by which to create a cohesive civilization. The idea that you cannot enter into heaven unless you attempt to practice these rules and give up your selfish nature to the idea that a divinity has been created to save you for eternity, give you salvation and an eternal life, is saying to me that allegiance to your soul is the entrance door to this eternal life. Whatever divinity exists, planted The Way into your soul. Be true to what it tells you and you're in. The Bible is a good guidebook to lead you through the quagmire of the competing emotions of greed, lust, love, and etcetera. Or if you subscribe to somebody like Voltaire who said, "If God did not exist, it would be necessary to invent him."

There is really no universal good and evil, no right and wrong. For every person there is a different set of laws by which he is bound. If you apply this concept it makes no sense to blame others for actions they have done to you. The perpetrators of those actions have their own rules with which to contend. So you can forget the casting of stones. But if you follow the rules of your own universe, you render any other person helpless to violate your universe. If they attempt such an action, you are perfectly just in crushing their efforts or at least making the attempt, if the actions they commit against you are contrary to the laws of your natural universe. If you go out of your universe and accept someone else's, then your personal God will dispense his justice. Whether an idea like this is contrary to basic Christian beliefs or not is not really relevant. If your personal universe is one and the same as The Lord, then his Rapture lights your way anyway. But if you accept the possibility that other people who may do things that are contrary to your own beliefs and determine that they are blameless, they live in their own personal universe, it is you who are to blame for allowing them to do it to you. Then, there is only one person you have to worry about changing. YOU. A lot of senseless emotions are avoided and you can move on.

The idea that some people were good and others evil can then be left to theologians and Saint Peter. Life may be short when you are old, but success, as well as failure, certainly is dynamic. A success achieved, or rather lived at an old age, may not be a poultice for events and people gone by, but as long as you breathe you still have your self-respect with which to deal. Feeling good about your present situation is a worthwhile pursuit. The past will always be there. There will be times you sit in a dark room and deal with that. Limiting those times by riding a snow machine through wonderland is maybe as expensive as lying on a couch in a dim room at the foot of some shrink's chair, but it is a lot more fun, and I think a lot more effective.

So, as long as we are dealing in personal universes, I have decided that words stated by Francis Bacon in the 1500s and paraphrased by the late John Bernard Books, deals with just what I'm talking about. Bacon: "...But above all, nothing conduces more to the well-representing of a man's self, and securing his own right, than not to disarm one's self by too much sweetness and good nature, which exposes a man to injuries and reproaches; but rather... at times to dart out some sparks of a free and generous mind, that have no less of the sting than the honey." Books is more pragmatic and far less polished in his view, but his philosophy is pretty sound, if somewhat hokey nowadays, and pretty much in line with Bacon.

Well now. The problem with being a man of average intelligence is that most of the secrets of the universe are entombed in intricate language or mathematics. So if you want to go beyond what the preachers tell you, then you have to go to the source of those secrets, or to those who contest or try to interpret the source. The Bible, philosophers, or if you choose, science. That's what I did. And where it got me was pretty much back to square one. But along the way I was able to come to my own conclusions, because in the life of a simple man, God will always find a way. I'm getting way ahead of myself, but I have given you a taste of what's in store for you. If you want to come along, do so. But if you choose to come along, keep in mind a couple of things. This book is about the perceptions I have come to, about two simple but profound states of mind. Spirituality or religion if you will. And depression; what I call demons. If you are looking for a well-researched divination or some sort of definitive dissertation on cause and effect, the latest medical or psychiatric information or a theological essay you have the wrong book. I have a basic distrust of clergy and psychiatry. At best, I am a bewildered layperson when it comes to science. I have no educational degrees beyond a high school diploma. What I have to offer is mostly empirical. That is, what I felt, saw and imagined.

William Styron is a favorite author. He resides in an intellectual bookcase about three shelves above me. Here is one of the things he had to say about depression in his book *Darkness Visible* "...that such madness is chemically induced amid the neurotransmitters of the brain, probably as the result of systemic stress, which for unknown reasons causes a depletion of the chemicals norepinephrine and serotonin, and the increase of a hormone, cortisol." You will find nothing of that sort here. If you choose to engage the blight of depression from the lofty heights of modern medicine and stratospheric intellect, read that book. If you want a novelized version of depression and near insanity, try *The Bell Jar* by Sylvia Plath. If you want to get down in the dirt and battle demons with a hillbilly, then come with me. I qualify that in one regard only. Philosophy started out as science and gradually morphed into metaphysics. What the hell is metaphysics? Webster's defines it as "The branch of philosophy dealing with first principles of things." Well that clears things up. Just so you know what I'm talking about, I'll give you my definition. Metaphysics are those emotions, processes, origins and questions that deal with the fundamental entity known as thought. Example: is thought a noun or a verb? A thing or a process? Philosophers for the most part were intellectuals in their day. And those guys wrote like they thought. So when I quote one of those guys, I simply try to interpret what they had to say into a like thought from my brain.

With that in mind, and if you are interested, hitch a ride with a hillbilly in a '65 Chevy pickup truck with no suspension, a 327 cubic inch engine and headers. It's a bumpy ride, but if you listen carefully, you may hear the heartbeat of that sweet little mill above all the noise.

I will now start at the beginning.

Chapter II
HER DARKENED DAYS

"Accept the things you cannot change.............."

T
he beginning takes me back to Fairbanks, Alaska to the year 1992. That is when I entered my new life with a true love. Modern times make modern marriages somewhat complicated. It was the second marriage for me the third for her. We had children and stepchildren between us that totaled six. Five alive and one dead.

He has stared at me from his place of prominence in the four houses that I have shared with Becky. He has always had a place of prominence. From that sacred place he stares at me. Blond hair and sparkling blue eyes frame the handsome young man. But it is his smile. His smile leaps from the photograph and permeates the room. It is a woman killer. It is a smile that speaks of joy from some mysterious source only partially revealed by the sky-blue eyes, because there is a hint of sadness in that smile. The glint of devilish charm from the crooked smile enraptures females from ten to eighty. The plaque that is also part of the shrine says, "Loving Son, GARY DION LOPES, 7-29-70 12-18-89." Dion, my stepson -- the one I never met.

Dion was the catalyst for the storm cloud that would pour rain into my life for a decade and more. Dion was the storm that would first block the sun and give life to the shadow that would gradually gain form and then substance. Becky and I came to call her that shadow, the Black Witch. Dion's death was the nourishment she fed on, the Black Witch. Becky's walk through that saddened valley, that valley of Dion's death, was pretty much alone. It is hard to know how to guide someone along the path of the Black Witch unless you have trod there yourself. That knowledge in itself is esoteric. I like words. Some have a texture and a feel, they sound cool. Then, once you learn their meaning, those words forever convey a visual image or a special condition or way of thinking or simply describe something more eloquently. "Esoteric" is such a word. Esoteric. "Religious, mystical or philosophical teaching or practice with a meaning that is understood only by those who have received the necessary instruction or training." Esoteric. Known to few. So it is that the Black Witch has such power. The few that have known her do not feel special. The few that have trod there have lost as many battles as they have won against that Black Witch. And they don't like to talk about it. So, the Black Witch, to me, is an esoteric travail through the darkened recesses of a deluded mind.

There are words that I like and there are those I do not like. "Soulmate" is a word I do not like. It is a tired and overused cliché. The image that springs to my brain when I see that word or hear it, is that there are all these deserving souls clattering around against other deserving souls. Instantly, like magic, a deserving soul finally encounters another like deserving soul. These incomplete deserving souls suddenly bond in a flash of blinding immaculation and become as one. I don't think anything could be further from the truth.

The process of falling in love, I would guess, is part of this mating of souls. That process starts by jumping in the front seat of the baddest roller coaster at Seven Flags. That first part, the courtship, is like that first ride. You climb slowly up that first big hill in rapt anticipation, and then plunge through a series of heart-stopping loops and turns. When you finally get back to the starting platform, you're all out of breath, in shock at the exhilaration of that first experience. Out of money and suffering a bit of post-courtship blues, you go home together. Now comes the test. I don't think that you can ever mate to another soul unless you are given the test.

Do you remember those cheap pens or lighters they made back in the 1960s? The ones with the girl in a swimming suit? You turn the lighter upside down and the swimming suit slowly drains away to reveal a naked body. That is the test. That's what happens when the wedding is over and everybody goes home. Over a period of months or years, each soul turns the other upside down and watches while the facade that was the courtship clothing, the courtship personality, slowly drains away. Then, you know what you've got. At that point, if you can look at each other and say, and mean it, "Not bad. We work together, we can make something out of you yet." Those two flawed and imperfect souls then do just that; they work together and try to make something out of the resulting whole. One slips, the other helps him back to his feet.

18

If one is full of bullshit, the other pulls the plug on that shit. You walk together in your resplendent garments through the parade of life. The other people in the parade see those splendid garments, but they are only seeing the emperor's clothes. You see each other as the naked, uncertain pilgrims that you really are. If there is a word that describes this process, it is not "soulmating." Then again, maybe I got it wrong. "Semantics" is another word I like. We could argue about that all day long.

My family jelled when I entered into a life with Becky. The process just described took a period of several years. Years in which Becky was ripped and torn in so many ways. When you enter into a life with another person, you need first to project the image of your soul, the honest image of yourself, onto the photo plates of that region of your brain that controls the analytical function process. Take several snapshots from all angles and study them carefully. When you marry another person, make sure that what you are looking for is a life mate and not something else. If you are looking for someone to cherish and polish that image you have of yourself, you are handing your partner the job of maid and servant. If you are that awesome, you don't need a mate, you only need to line all your rooms with full-length mirrors. If you need a person to justify and validate your life, you don't need a mate, you need a preacher. If you need a body to satisfy your carnal nature and to display as a trophy, you don't need a mate; you need a high-class call girl. If you need only a nurturing womb to provide you with offspring, you need to hire a surrogate.

The image I projected on to the screen of my intelligence was, I think this time, the right one. I was looking for a mate when I found Becky. But of course we had to go through the disappearing swimming suit process while we learned about each other. What Becky found after all those years will be left unrecorded. What I found was a wounded soldier of infinite compassion, who was in love with me. I found a woman with weaknesses enough to match my own. But as her swimming suit drained away, it stopped just short of completely naked. I waited, but no more; that was it. It was such a narrow band, that hidden part, that I wrote it off as insignificant. But that last little part was vitally important. That last band concealed those parts of her soul that will never be known to any mortal. But also in there were some tragic events that would never be reconciled. Things that were un-reconcilable. Things that were unchangeable. Things that were unacceptable. But also, there was the knowledge there that her mate, me, was responsible for taking a few careless potshots and contributing to those wounds that she carried like a soldier, on most days.

My own family encompasses the product of five marriages. Of all that progeny, there is only one kid that is pretty much a blank spot in my brain. A rain cloud forms when conditions are right for its creation. The humidity and the temperature of the air must be just right. But for a raindrop to form, there must be a speck of dust, a particle of some kind that the moisture can adhere to, a catalyst for rain to form around. Dion was that speck of dust, that catalyst for the rain cloud to form around, that so darkened her days. Dion. Just as Dion was approaching full manhood, he was killed. Killed in a car accident under dubious circumstances. Becky will never reconcile that event. She will live with it.

I entered Becky's life shortly after this sad event. I entered it on a fulltime basis. I had toyed with our relationship for a time for selfish reasons of my own. I entered it now, a blundering knight, not so much white, as opaque. The Opaque Knight. I couldn't see through my shaded self and see what she really needed. My vision was staring straight ahead, wasn't looking at her at all. I wasn't looking to see, to try and understand my beautiful wife. I saw things as through a shaded glass, always shaded towards me.

In rapid succession, things began to get ripped and torn from Becky's life. After the death of Dion, her life-giving was torn from her. Fairbanks Memorial tore her womb from her. Her eldest son left us then. Her other son, Jeremy left on a mission of his own; his own life. I soon tore her away from her only real home of the last decade and deposited her in an alien city, just on the outskirts of Alaska. Anchorage. This final insult, why? Having already failed at consecutive businesses, I was convinced the third time was a charm. Lost in all of this folly was the realization that all these events were leveled at the crosshairs of Becky's sanity. I stumbled blindly on, berating Becky for her dour moods. The fabric of our marriage was being stretched to its limit. In ignorance and self-pity, my lecturing and whining were like manure being dumped on the damp, dark soil of her un-reconciled underground, where only parasites grow. That tiny, unrevealed nakedness, that final sliver of swimming suit, that last, most naked part of her soul, was fertile ground for the blight of the Black Witch.

So let's leave Becky here for a minute and let's talk about the Opaque Knight. The Opaque Knight had lived a helluva life. The world had been his oyster. He had traveled widely, done many exotic and exciting things. He had never lost, only won. He was bulletproof with an ego to match. But what the Opaque Knight did not know, was that he had never really been tested. Five-foot, three-inches of Strawberry Blonde Enigma would forever rust the armor of the Opaque knight.

I spent five years with the blonde enigma. Sherry brought a son into my life as part of the deal. We sealed the deal with a little blonde enigma that was my very own. Ben and Tasha. Reason enough for those lost days with the Strawberry Blonde Enigma.

Women have a distinct advantage over men when it comes to recognizing and identifying the substance and nature of their emotions. Men tend to emphasize the practical side of the reality of their own lives and the times they are passing through. Women demand that their emotions be attended to. Men try to avoid the reality that they even exist. This apparent irony is well known to all men of a certain age, that lust being the one emotion young men demand receive some attention. As is most things in my life, things that went wrong were for the most part, my own damn fault. The pieces of the puzzle of our demise were in place from the beginning. All it took was someone who recognized the fact and started pushing the pieces into a discernable picture. Once the first pieces were in place, the rest started flying together of their own volition. The catalyst of course was that we simply did not know how to love each other. We were not willing to sacrifice personal feelings for someone we were not ready to love.

This process took about five years. To her credit, Sherry recognized the end when it was approaching and was strong enough to not further cloud the situation. She made it clear how she felt. Feelings she had buried, now finally demanded attention. She hated the life here in the north and she wanted to go home.

All this is a simplification. I, in full confidence of my abilities, had quit my job and started a business with two friends. To those of you uninitiated, business and friendship are mutually exclusive, at least when things go bad. As events would later prove, where money is involved, when the propagation of money or the propagation of a friendship are put on the same table and you can only grab one or the other, the importance of each becomes perfectly clear. Since we went into business to make money, I hold no ill will. I survived this business relationship with one friendship intact, and learned more about the nature of words and human nature. All this is of course tempered with blame. The most important thing I learned from this whole experience is one simple fact -- all people of any ambition tend to take a higher view of their own importance than of those around them. Me included. In my mom's words, "If you could buy him for what he is worth, and sell him for what he thinks he's worth, you would never have to work another day."

In 1985 we started our business. That same year the economy of the state of Alaska went into steep decline along with the price of oil, upon which Alaska's economy is very dependent. Our business staggered along with my personal income. Sherry was caught in the middle of all this, along with a deep distrust of one of my partners. When the economy and my income collapsed, it set up a series of events that precipitated the foreclosure of our house. I found myself broke, deeply in debt and my personal life in shambles. It is a situation that would remain with me all, or in part, for the next fifteen years.

The breakup of a marriage is a terrible thing. The breakup of a family is a devastating thing. Imposing a space of twenty-five hundred miles between you and your kids causes several things to happen. All of a sudden you have a lot of time you never had before. Suddenly your position of role model has evaporated. The hurt and the question of your manhood are brought sharply into focus. Throw in a failing business, living in the basement of your business and the dark and cold of Fairbanks in the wintertime and you have a recipe for illusions and delusions.

My family was finally and forever gone. Gone as far as me ever being part of their family unit was concerned. Some men would have knuckled down. Others would have gone on a search for a new family. Some may have embarked on a search of a spiritual nature. I went on a search and destroy mission. Search for trouble and the destruction of me. There are few married couples in existence that have not at one time or other approached the precipice of divorce. If love exists in the hearts of both parties, there is a reasonable chance they will step back and reclaim that marriage. If love does not exist in one or both parties, and there are no extenuating circumstances to sustain the union, it is doomed.

Of course the kids are another matter altogether. Looking back with the advantage of objectivity gained over the contemplation of fifteen years, it was the kids, or the loss of them in everyday life that was the real destructive factor in the way I conducted myself. Their presence precluded the possibility of most of my indulgence into destructive behavior.

I was thirty-five years old and I had never failed at anything. In the space of a year I had lost my family, I had lost my retirement, I had lost all my assets at the financial and the emotional level. The only thing I was in search of was a respite from the horrors living in my head. You have heard this story before. Alcohol. Cocaine.

The very night that my wife left for good, I started drinking. And my partner thought it would be a good idea for me to try some cocaine. So I did. An eight ball they called it in those days. So, I drank and I drank some more. A little cocaine. I truly was a legend in my own mind. Then I drank some more because I could not sleep. A little cocaine. I drank for a week because I could not sleep. Then I ran out of cocaine. Sleep came easy then.

When I next woke, it was to a hangover the like of which I had never experienced before or since. I had nothing with which to compare it. When several hours went by and my body continued to shake and the paranoia in my head went from mild to severe, I got to the point of considering checking myself into the emergency room. It was like I was riding a wave of panic, and the more I tried not to think about it, the worse it got. I surfed there uncertainly for one whole day. I expected at any time to lose my head and go crashing down the face of that wave and get slammed into the coral reef that I was sure lay beneath. When that wave finally crashed, I was a total mess. No money, no wife, no kids, and now no alcohol. Cocaine was not an option; no money.

What a load of drivel. I was a skid row drunk. Everything was much grander on the way up the wave, even more dramatic on the way down. My normal, self-deprecating nature was elevated by chemicals, as to be living a great drama. Lowlife drunk, whining pie-eyed hangover. Drugs really do suck.

So, I learned about the nature of drugs, not that I didn't already know that story. This is an old story and deserves no further mention. Of course, had I any sense at all, I would have avoided the process of trying to re-examine the excesses of youth and I would have continued to concentrate on my family and the business. The emasculation of the sense of who you are, your worth and your future, is a slow and insidious process. The thought that the remedy would be a kind and gentle process was never considered. To think that it might take ten years and test the limits of my ability and the inquisition of my spirit, was inconceivable. That was just as well. Had I known that simple fact, I would have simply given up.

During those dark days that followed, I was simply left to lament the good times and dwell endlessly on what character defect, what part of my manhood, was suspect. You see, I had all the time in the world because I couldn't sleep. Not at all, not for days on end. You combine a steady intake of alcohol, constant fatigue and the brutality of solitude, you have set yourself up for not only delusions; you have also set yourself to be manipulated. Manipulated by your own mania and those around you, be their intentions pure or otherwise. And you are forced to relive in great detail those things best dumped into the trash bin of rationalization. Deep inside you know this is all very melodramatic, but you simply have no answers. You are incarcerated in a prison of your own construction. You drink more and sleep less. Each day brings a new crises. You know something has to break and you hope it won't be your spirit.

What little joy that you have left is remembering those times you get to spend with your kids. Your daughter is just three. Her innocence is a thing to hold on to, until that too turns into a black fist that grips your heart. On a sunny day at the park, just the two of you, she calls you by the name of your wife's boyfriend. Several times. You now have been completely whipped. No sleep, only time to think, not think, speculate with a ravaged brain soaked in alcohol. Then is when you should start the process of rebuilding. But when there is nothing of value, what do you grasp on to, when there is nothing to hold on to?

So, you set off on a journey of tearing things down. In the process, you find that you still have the ability to hurt. You can spread around the misery. So you do. Meanwhile the dominos continue to fall. The crashing economy sends others you call friends back down to their other lives -- the ones they had before they came to Alaska. The thought of returning to my old life is unacceptable. Knowing full well that you have no faith in your ability, no faith in your business, simply no faith, you just persevere.

It is at this juncture where you can get into serious trouble. To this point, you have been sustained by your emotions and alcohol. The rending of the family has left you with plenty of emotions to keep you occupied. Once you get past this first, all emotional stage, once the possibility of physical violence has passed, you are only at the first step in what's to be a long, debilitating journey. Then comes the payback stage. Since striking out directly at the ex-wife only hurts the kids, you strike elsewhere. If you are looking, you will find a lot of potential targets. Once you have punched other peoples' emotions around and gain no solace, now you have arrived at a bad juncture. If you can escape this minefield, then you think you are invulnerable. You've taken life's best shots and given some back. Bring it on.

Knowledge is where you find it. The source of knowledge is irrelevant. A truth, as it applies to that most cherished of all possessions, the acquisition of insight, is of itself, invaluable. A simple statement. Turn the other cheek. A very useful lesson. When you get hammered by life, and I'm not talking about someone belting you in a bar -- that's something else. But when you really get hammered, if at that point you have the courage to accept what you cannot change and not rail against it, you will save yourself precious years. I wasted precious years in the childhood of my children, raging against the machine. In this rage is where your worst mistakes are bound to happen.

The worst thing about living in a delusion is that, guess what? You don't realize it at the time. But at a time when I was striking back, I completely forgot who I was. I imagined myself to be a worldly man with a past. What I was, was a pathetic puppet. I was dancing to my own inadequacy and an image I had of myself that was what I thought I should be at this stage in my life. The fact was, that I was not that man. I was a broken down icon of my past success, a legend in my own mind. So ignoring the truth, I set myself up to entertain any idea that would further that lie. I was susceptible to any outside provocation that would improve my self-image or enrich me. It was at this juncture that I could have damaged my life or my conscience beyond repair. I even took a step or two down this road. Consequences are something that you have to deal with only if you lose. Don't believe it for a second. I can only say that good luck and the possibility of having to face my mother stayed the flow of these bad ideas. Had I turned the other cheek, and dealt with the problem in the first place, I would have saved myself many sleepless nights and distasteful morning inspections in the mirror. In the end, I discovered that in any pursuit of a spiritual nature, cause and effect are irrelevant. If spirituality exists, it resides within you from day one. You cannot create spirituality by being good, you can't destroy it by being bad, you can only discover that you have possessed it all along, and if you ever find it, then the nature of it becomes apparent, the pathway to its enhancement, obvious. The idea of reliving your life to salvage your soul by rectifying mistakes is really just the reverse. You are sanctimoniously listing your accomplishments now that your legacy has been tarnished, and holding up only those few "regrets" in some sort of perverse balance sheet of your net worth.

What was the problem, then, in the first place? I guess that depends on your view of the world. If you think that the world is a test for an afterlife, then the problem was that I had no faith. If you think the world is an uncompromising jungle where the strong survive, I choose to think I was a wounded dog; a hard-working sheep dog maybe. If you choose to think that the world is a dynamic, chaotic storm of unrelated emotional and physical collisions, then I would have to say that I had just gotten bounced hard off the side-rail and was spinning slowly towards the corner pocket. Whatever the reality, there was nothing to prevent me from dusting off the dirt and looking for a shower. But then I didn't turn the other cheek -- I bounced off the floor and attacked the wall in the dark. Had I stopped and looked for a light I would have known the door was three feet away. All I had to do was turn on the light. Look around with my facilities as well-tuned as I could make them, and go on. People who have been in a similar situation might say that that is a load of crap. Maybe so. There are Vietnam vets with artificial legs who ended up swallowing a gun into an afterlife. There are Vietnam vets who are in a wheelchair and end up heading the VA. It was a load of crap for one guy, not for the other. Depends on your perspective.

But for all the rhetoric, the dominos continued to fall. Five years I spent in exile from my kids and my family. A brief experiment at reconciliation was a farce, but allowed me time with the kids. Finally, I was ready to find a door out of the dark room. Our business finally failed for reasons that are important only in a few regards. It terminated a relationship that was very unhealthy for both parties involved. It clarified my financial situation so I had a starting point, and ultimately it forced me to leave Fairbanks.

Two things happened in the early 1990's to change my life in a positive way. The door out of the dark room was lit by the smile of a beautiful woman. Rebecca had been in my life for seven years when we finally got married. The other, the Hercules aircraft came flying back into my life after an absence of half a decade. There were to be plenty of negative forces at work also.

My wife Becky is one of the kindest and most loving people ever to inhabit my sphere of awareness. In order to be this type of person, you have to possess a high degree of sensitivity. In that one sense, we were light years apart. This difference in our personality would be the only real hammer that could wedge spikes between us.

Two years before we were married, she lost Dion. A woman's emotions, and how she deals with them, are a mystery that I believe is impenetrable to the standard-issue male's brain. There has to be a formative difference. No other explanation, or so it seemed at the time.

The devastation she suffered would linger beyond my means to understand. My stupid attempt to reconcile with my ex-wife, had consequences that took years for me to understand. What it all added up to was that when we finally got married in the spring of 1992, there were as they say, unresolved issues. The ultimate demise of our business added to the issues. When the Herc came flying back into my life, that too was a double-edged sword.

The Lockheed Hercules is a huge four-engine, cargo aircraft. It can operate on practically any runway of a length of over thirty-five hundred feet. It can carry cargo weighing nearly fifty thousand pounds. It was the main form of air transportation of equipment during the construction of the Alaskan pipeline. I had grown up on it. From 1973 until 1985, I spent my entire working life in the back of this wonderful airplane. I had traveled to uncounted foreign countries on five different continents. When the nature of the business in Alaska changed and the Herc was being faded out, I faded out as well and that's when we started our ill-fated business.

That all changed when Southern Air Transport showed up on my doorstep. Southern Air has an early history combined of smoke and mirrors as they say. CIA air as some called it. However, that had all changed in recent years and they had bought the Hercs of my former company, Alaska International Air/Markair. They were coming to Alaska and needed some loadmasters. I needed a job. It was a good fit. I, along with two men whom I had worked with in the past, formed a company to do the ground handling for SAT in Fairbanks and Anchorage. I had finally become what I always wanted to be, a double-dipper. I made money working for SAT and also from our little ground handling company. There was a price to pay. We had to move from Fairbanks to Anchorage, as that was where most of the action was.

Something happened just prior to our moving that caused me to begin the process of understanding Becky and the debilitating ghost she was dealing with in the death of her son. My mother died.

My mother had a single purpose in life. That was her kids; all ten of them. My mother led two lives after she was married. One with her husband. They married in 1933. During WWII they left the farm in Minnesota and moved to Vancouver, Washington. They worked in the shipyards and prospered to some degree after the war. My dad was a carpenter of some skill. For a while, he made a good living. He then went to work for the state. Life was pretty good. The last child was born in 1956. My dad was a fun-loving, hard-drinking man. Today, after having been a parent, I can begin to understand the pressures he must have been under, having at least eight kids to feed. My oldest brother and sister were on their own by this time. It is said by two of the older siblings that he was a wonderful father. That, then, is the first of the two lives my mother was to live. Dad was a good provider a good husband, a good dad. In the late 1950's this all changed.

When dad got the state job, he spent a lot of time on the road. He liked drinking, he liked to have fun. So he started having fun in bars on the road. The detailed history of this time is unknown to us younger kids, but it's not hard to figure out.

About 1960 my mom had had enough and told him to leave and not come back. At the age of fifty she had few saleable skills, still had six kids at home and no income. This began a period of near poverty and tough times. She took jobs where she could find them, usually working as a maid in the homes of rich folks. She scammed the ADC folks (Aid to Dependent Children) by getting paid in cash for this manual labor. We moved about six times between the time I was ten and when I finally graduated.

In those days, divorce was not nearly as prevalent as today. Most of the schools we went to, I couldn't name another kid who didn't have a dad. My mom, or Granny, as we called her, performed all parental functions. We always ate well, we all played whatever sports we wanted, we took vacations. I can remember one time when we were to be evicted from where we were living at the time. My mom faced down the landlord and the county sheriff's deputy in the front yard. They left. When we were old enough, starting about age twelve, we picked beans in the summer to earn our school clothes. My mom, then in her mid-fifties, was there with us from six in the morning until three or four in the afternoon. She did this until the summer she got hurt in a car accident, about 1965. On a good day, if we picked two hundred pounds, we made $5.00 apiece.

The older my mom got, the stronger she got. When I was about sixteen, she got a job at the state agency of Head Start. We all got other summertime jobs and the bean fields became a memory. The years after I graduated were generally better for her and she was able to live in dignity.

My mom died after an on again, off again battle with cancer. When it finally became apparent that she was not going to make it, I got a call from Al, my sister's husband. The thought of dealing with this was almost unbearable to me. But she had become increasingly ill, and for all concerned I'm sure it was the best thing. She never wanted to be a burden, and those were not idle words.

The funeral was like all funerals. When it was over we came home. As time goes by I come to realize that, personal prejudice aside, she was a very special person. My regard for her continues to grow as I am confronted with the vagaries of life. Here is a small thing of great importance that I learned from my mom and that some kids never learn. I learned it through hard times. If you never have hard times you might not understand this. If your parents truly love you, the things they tell you are the truth as they know it. You may go through your entire life and have only those things your parents try to teach you as unadulterated, pure, un-distilled advice, free from any ulterior motive. If you think about it, you will find that whatever advice you may get along the path of life, everyone you come into contact with may have an ulterior motive for whatever they say to you. Be it your friend, your wife, your banker, whoever. If your parents love you, what they tell you, whether it be right or wrong, is the un-distilled truth as they understand it. Once they are gone, it is possible that you will never get another chance to hear the complete truth from another human being.

You may have to consider all information from that point forward, as someone else's bias. Finding someone you can trust unconditionally is a mighty task.

When we left for Anchorage, Becky was dealing with her dead son. I was dealing with the loss of my mother. Becky had become ill. When the Fairbanks doctors were done with her, we were an additional $30,000 in debt, she was minus her female organs and deeply depressed, but she had quit smoking. We moved into an apartment on the edge of an upscale ghetto in Anchorage. We were still in the throes of shutting down our previous company. It was a time of fear of a phone call, fear of getting the mail. But with Southern Air we were making enough money to get by. In spite of our best efforts, the sun began to set on my job with SAT and the life of our little ground handling company. It would be an additional two years before this became manifest.

During this two-year period, we were able to slowly get a handle on our debt. Becky was unable to accept that she was in the grip of depression. The existence of this condition is not in question. The nature of depression is still not agreed upon by the medical community. The treatment is varied and much debated.

But this is all academic. Becky was sure it was just the fact that she had been torn from her home in Fairbanks, her last son was out of the house and the fact that she had no job that was causing her to be so unhappy. Who could argue with that? She said it would soon pass.

Becky's home in Fairbanks was an ideal for kids and a guy like me. She had a sanctuary that took up the bedroom. The rest of the house was for the world. Becky's friends, my friends, Jeremy's friends would gather around the table all days of the week and all hours of the day. We would laugh and talk. There was always an extra kid around, spending the night or being babysat. It was a communal campground that was full of life, but maybe short of Martha Stewart's ideal of housekeeping. She had friends that you couldn't count on two hands. Becky's brother and his wife and kids lived in Fairbanks. Becky's house sat on a quiet street, a short walk to the Chena River. She knew the neighbors on all sides, had watched the neighbor kids grow up. During the summers it was a free-for-all when Tasha and Ben would come and spend a month or so. Tasha was my daughter and Ben my stepson.

From here I took her to a two-bedroom "townhouse" set in a duplex in the middle of twenty duplexes exactly the same as ours, on a street that was the entry road for the ghetto that lay beyond. She had no friends, no job, and just before leaving Fairbanks, had a carpel tunnel surgery. I couldn't understand why she was unhappy. Oh, did I mention we were broke? The male seems to have a huge capacity for pushing unpleasant little facts into a convenient dark corner of the mind. Women seem to have to live in a world where every unpleasant fact is transformed into an emotional issue. That issue is then the object of an individual spotlight that shines on the stage of our life. Our stage was lit by a lot of spotlights. All those spotlights blinded me. They served to light up Becky's sleepless nights and illuminate each individual problem in the minutest detail. Then, of course there was Dion.

Dion was Becky's second oldest son. He had died in a car crash in California. Becky had been unable to attend the funeral. I never met Dion, but I got to know him quite well. The tragedy was made worse because of the circumstances of the accident. No details are necessary. It is only important to say that the events around his death were suspicious and never resolved.

During this time, there were days when I would come home and find Becky crying alone in our bedroom. There was never any reason, she always said, but later, more often than not, I would find out that it involved a certain date on which a certain event concerning Dion had taken place in the past. Of course, the dates that fell upon those of his birth and death were the hardest for Becky to bear. She would anticipate those dates and the deepest, darkest days would be in advance of, and during those particular days. This first winter in Anchorage tested the strength of our relationship. The tragedy for me was getting to know this blond-haired young man who smiled out at me from his place on the TV. I learned intimate details of his life and I was able to make my own judgments from the devil in his eyes and the humor of his smile. I never got to meet him.

The winter finally ended. The girls showed up along with the sun of summer. It was apparent that our little business needed to be expanded or closed. We continued on. The girls, my daughter, Tasha and my niece, Rachael, were best friends. When they showed up to spend some time with us, Becky was reborn. Her mood, state of mind, or depression, whatever you choose to call it, was like an evil spell that she was able to vanquish for periods of time. But this witch of gloom did not go away. Not entirely. She would jump at will from the closet where Becky kept her. Becky did not have a lock on that closet. For the most part, the days were great. Becky had two kids. The girls, I think, were about fourteen at the time. A sticky time for young ladies. And Becky was a convenient mother. The two girls turned a blind eye whenever the witch would appear. Becky had a lot of good days with them.

Later, Jeremy and Ben came to stay for a time. The summers made the rest bearable. We took our old motorhome and went fishing and clamming. These two dudes were about nineteen then. So they took the truck and went to Fairbanks to see their buddies. But we both loved it when the kids were there and, for a short time at least, didn't worry about much; let the credit cards roll.

But summer ended and it started to get dark, and the Witch was anxious. Becky's brother Tom came to stay with us. He was going to school in Anchorage for the winter and we loved having him there. He helped with expenses and Becky would try to keep the Witch at bay when Tom was there. Then the Seattle Mariners did a wonderful thing. They beat the Angels in a one game playoff and got into baseball's postseason. Tom is to sports fan what fat is to cholesterol. We sat around the TV every night that the Mariners were playing. We enjoyed an orgy of elation when they beat the hated Yankees. When the Mariners finally succumbed to the bought-and-paid-for Indians, it was OK. That winter Tommy, the vole and Backstrap made the winter bearable.

As soon as it got cold, the vole moved in with us. A vole is a tiny mouse-like rodent. He surprised Becky one day in the laundry room and sealed his doom in the process. We got some traps from the hardware store and the game was on. He eluded us for a week. We came home one day to find the vole hung in effigy on our door with a note of warning to his brethren. Tom one, voles nothing.

Backstrap was a yearling moose that liked to hang out in our front yard, back yard, across the street- -- wherever, and eat the leaves from the shrubs. Any time you came home late at night you had to beware of Backstrap. A couple of times we would be walking in the pitch dark and come upon him suddenly. He was a young moose, but still, he was six or seven hundred pounds of scared beast and liable to do anything. That winter a man at the university was trampled to death after surprising a moose. We evaded Backstrap that winter and spring was coming.

The journey to understanding a woman is like walking down a path with that woman and the path is strewn with flowers. Each flower is one you have seen before, but you don't know the name. Why? Well, because flowers have always been like window dressing for the path through the woods. The real important stuff was the trees and the wild animals. Flowers are important too, and every man should learn their names. The biggest and most beautiful flower on Becky's path was named "children." If you learn all about that flower and cultivate it with her, you can touch her heart. But you can only touch it. If you want to hold her heart, you still must learn about the rest of her flowers. Of course this path dips out of sight ahead of you, appears a half mile or so up ahead, before it drops out of sight on the horizon. It's lined the entire length with flowers you have seen before, but you don't know their names. If she picks a flower and shows it to you, look at it, discover its beauty, find out the name of that flower.

The flower she held in her hand that spring was the one called "home." I had lived most of my adult life in places. I had never had a home since I had left my mother's home. I am sure that is part of the reason for the failure of my first marriage. My domestic surroundings had been important only in the matters of shelter and a place to park my airplane.

Anchorage is a city of a couple hundred thousand people. It is located in a beautiful setting. The Chugach Mountains rise as a backdrop to the east. The town is pretty well surrounded by water on the other three sides. The view out of our window was wall-to-wall duplexes. Those beautiful mountains might as well have been covered in clouds year around. The Black Witch had been at bay most of that winter. Tom had a lot to do with that. Tom had finished school and was leaving soon. Becky was working at our company. We couldn't afford to pay Becky, but it got her out of the house.

We had made progress in tying up loose ends on our business in Fairbanks. We had made some headway in clearing up most of the collection agency debts and between my two jobs had gotten at least stable. Becky's parents are wonderful people. Both had worked a lifetime and were now in the stage where they could savor some of the fruits of their success. As a result of their careful planning and hard work, they were now able to share some of that success with their three children. This money was indispensable to us. With the help of our bank in Fairbanks, we were able to wade through the morass of late payments and bounced checks with a semblance of dignity.

So, one spring day, just for the hell of it, we went looking for a new place to live. We found a place for rent overlooking a lake that had floatplanes on it and best of all, the entire front window on the upper level was a picture frame for the Chugach Mountains. Becky lit up like the aurora when she walked to the window in the living room and stared out at the mountains. We took the place and Tom helped us move in before he left that spring for his home in Fairbanks.

The Black Witch came with us. Becky moved her into the garage. The Witch left us alone most of that summer. Tasha and Rachael came to stay for a month. They loved the place. Ben and Jeremy came too and the summer was great while the Witch slept in the garage. Tasha was fifteen that summer. What a terrible time it must be for a girl nowadays at that age. Both girls were dieting. Tasha had the big bones of her Scandinavian heritage. I would watch her when she and Rachael took their walks around the block. The weight she carried on her frame looked so unnatural that you knew that in order for her to keep it down to that level, she would have to starve herself. Her natural beauty would only blossom if she let her natural weight return. No way. But she and Rachael were a delight for us that summer.

The summer passed and the Black Witch woke up. That fall and winter was a test of wills between Becky and the Black Witch. We left the Witch at home over the holidays when the kids came up for Christmas. We had a great time at the Alyeska resort. Tasha, Ben and Jeremy plus girlfriends, nieces, nephews and friends joined us. Life has a way of changing as kids grow up and go their own way. This was to be the last time we would all be together.

Chapter III

MY DARKENED DAYS

"How unfair that you should leave without
even a good-bye." Rachael Scott

A wonderful thing happened that early spring. Southern Air Transport decided to get into the passenger business. At the bequest of the military, Southern Air decided to make a combi version of two of their airplanes. A combi is an aircraft that carries both passengers and cargo. There were no such Hercules in existence. So, Southern Air designed the modification, built it and got it certified by the military and the FAA. The military wanted to use this aircraft to operate between their bases in Europe and from Japan. Becky was offered a job as a flight attendant. She had to go to Columbus for training, but she was elated. A funny thing happened then. Becky drove a stake into the heart of that Black Witch.

Becky had been gone a week. She usually called once a day. I was sitting at my desk at the airport when the phone rang. Expecting it to be Becky, I picked it up ready with a smart remark. Some woman, whose voice I did not recognize, asked me if I was Steve Scott. I said I was and she asked me to hold on for a minute. The next voice that came on the line was of my ex-wife, Sherry. She was in a state of hysteria. She finally stammered out the words that Tasha had been in an accident and she broke into sobs. I told her to calm down and just tell me how bad it was. For a period of perhaps twenty seconds she continued to sob uncontrollably. Then she said these two words. "She's deeeaad." Two words. A door swung wide open to reveal a universe changed forever on the hinge of two words.

Sometime later I found myself across the room, slammed up against the wall. The phone was still in my hand. I had somehow levitated from the chair at my desk, traveled eight feet across the room and now lay on the floor, back against the wall. I threw the offending phone away and sat there, stunned. Wolfman, Gene, our supervisor, stood at the door of my office. Our exchange was brief and to the point. He appeared about three minutes later with a water glass of whiskey, asked what he could do. I simply shook my head and he went away.

The goddamned phone started ringing again. Gene picked it up, appeared at the door a minute later and said that I had to talk on the phone. I did. I hung up and drank the whiskey. I made four more phone calls. That's all I could do. I went home, or Gene took me home. I ended up at home. I have no recollection of the rest of that day.

Interlude with Sherry, part one

"Take another piece of my heart..." Janis Joplin

So who says the world can't end? That bitch sitting across the table? And what the f... does she know? I'm a religious catholic girl. No I'm not a nice girl. I've done some drugs, I've hurt some people, and made some mistakes. I ain't pure, but I'm a good girl and I don't deserve this shit. When my time comes, I'm ready for that, I'm strong enough for that. I can't handle this shit. Where the hell is my Rosary? Now the bitch has her mouth open. God dammit, can't she just leave me alone? Doesn't she know I'm dying here?

"God dammit, just leave me alone, you don't know what is happening. This can't be happening. Please tell me that it isn't happening."

Some asshole has his arms around me. God dammit, please.........."Oh Tasha, Tasha, no, no..."NO!!!!"

I came awake slowly. I was drowsy, they had given me something. God this can't be real.

"The hell with you God, the hell with you."

I looked over and Bill was sitting there. He was sitting there with his head down. I reached over and grabbed his hand. "Can you get me something so I can go to sleep?" He looked up, he'd been crying. He nodded, got up and left.

I thought about it for a few minutes. I wanted to die. No one knows what that feels like.

Sometime the next day, my brother-in-law Tommy showed up. He would be one of the most sensible people I came into contact with over the next couple of weeks. He said, "I have nothing to say, except I'm sorry. I don't know what you are going through. What can I do to help?" My flight to Seattle didn't leave until midnight. Tommy allowed me to buy one six-pack of beer. Then we got the hell out of town. How anyone can deal with desolation in a big city is a wonder to me. It only takes about fifteen minutes to put Anchorage out of sight. The Turnagin Arm and the road that forms three sides of it provide a spectacular vista of mountains. In March, when the tide is out, the frozen chunks of ice, some as large as pickup trucks, cling to the shoreline. The giant shapes of ice are formed from tide action that rushes in, eroding and molding, melting and shaping. Then the tide recedes and the resulting landscape is like that of the moon viewed through a telescope. You can imagine anything you want, driving along this ever-changing alien land.

Drinking beer, your mind is unable to reason, only to reflect. At first it is a film reel. Tasha as a baby. Tasha as a two-year-old, eating pickles like her dad at Pike's. Tashsa being flung into the air as high as you could throw her, laughing with a joy like spring rain. A two-year-old Tasha walking up the stairs at the airport, defying Dad's warnings not to do so. Tasha in your arms as you run at full speed for your truck after you picked her up where she lay on the pavement after the car hit her, her bike mangled in the ditch. Tasha the defiant young lady after Ben and Jeremy found her and brought her home from a party when she was barely fourteen. Tasha the young lady, schmoozing her dad for a trip to the mall. A thousand other visions.

I glanced out the window constantly. I tried to maintain this bitter sweetness. Sadness was like a bandage. The bandage kept the gut shot, the raw void, the truth at bay. Tom was silent. We drove until I had only three beers left and we turned around. We started back to Anchorage. I kept those truths at bay. We finally drove through the marsh and the city came into view. The city. I needed more alcohol. Tommy relented. I somehow never let those thoughts in that day, nor for many days to come. I never had to witness it. I never had to see the body lying in a cubicle -- I never did. The really terrible thoughts came much later. I was to meet Becky and some members of my family in Seattle.

To those of you who do not have a family I can only offer you my deepest sympathy. I took care of nothing but found myself on an airplane with Bernie, my partner next to me. We were in first class and we were heading for Seattle. Bernie is about as sentimental as the rear bumper of an Edsel. He was my perfect traveling companion. Somehow the support group had erected a barrier to keep me from seeing or thinking about too much. We drank whiskey and joked about the deathwatch. I was a hard and able man.

When we got to Seattle, I went on ahead. There were about five of my family members and one friend who had driven to Seattle. They surrounded me, literally and figuratively, like a wall. When I lost it and broke down sobbing they pushed me up against a wall and formed a barrier around me. A barrier between me and all those faces in that terrible city, on that terrible day.

That day was a glazed-over time of things that had to be done. My family took care of all those things. We went and saw Sherry and more things were decided. Becky finally showed up and we were able to get on the road to Vancouver. We arrived in the early evening. We went to my brother's house. All of my family, save those who were en-route, were at my brother's house. There were spouses and there were a few good friends there also.

Interlude with Sherry, part two

*"It means she's lost the will to live, and I'm so
lonesome I could cry." Woody Guthrie.*

Well, he looks like he's doing better than me. Got his whole family, they were always tight, I'll give him that. Where the hell is my family? Bet my goddamn brother won't even show. I got Bill, I got Ben, Barb is here, dad will show. Thank God I got Justin, what would I do if I didn't have Justin? And Suki. Man, I just don't know if I can handle this. I got up and and went to the pill bottle by the nightstand. "Well God at least you gave me this shit." "What the hell am I going to do? I can't even look at myself in the mirror. I can see her in my eyes. Her eyes, the shadow of them staring back at me from my face. She's only been gone a few days. I can't stand this. I could have done so many things different. She could be sitting over there right now giving me shit about drinking too much. Telling me that I could cut my hair different. Showing me that poem that Rachael sent her. Her eyes all full of life. Talking about Jared and snowboarding with all her friends, wanting them all to spend the night at the river house in Baring. No, she's laying on a slab of concrete somewhere with some asshole cutting out her stomach to see if she was doing some drugs or some shit. And I got to deal with the insurance company and the poor kid who was driving the car that Tasha was riding in, and his parents. I hate that little bastard and I feel so sorry for him, but God I feel sorry for myself and I can't help it and I don't know what to do. "Oh Tasha, why? God damnit why?" I was screaming and crying and I just didn't know if I could make it.

The bitter sweetness, the blanket, had worked to sooth my mind like a salve. Finally, after two full days, I was home and I let that salve melt away. I didn't need to pretend anymore. So they, all of them, had to bear the brunt of my tragedy. Our tragedy. My main memory is sitting in a chair, my head in my hands, elbows on my thighs. My heart dissolved into tears and rained down on the carpet below. Then it broke. I had held, only partially conscious of it, a hot sea of emotion behind a dike of slowly melting ice. That dike now gave way. The person sitting in front of me changed every few minutes. I fired out my hurt as from a quiver of many poison arrows. One after another, in unmeasured intervals. Whoever occupied the chair opposite me, absorbed those poisoned barbs and offered common sense in return. But there was no common sense. There was no sense of any kind. There was only the hurt.

Then I had to go back to Seattle. Becky, Rachael, Jeremy and I drove to Seattle. It had been agreed to bury Tasha next to her grandmother in Vancouver. We had to go to Seattle to attend the ceremony that was being held in Tasha's honor at a church north of Seattle. The entire school was to attend. We arranged to meet Ben and his mother at a restaurant. Ben was there, his mother was not. We waited as long as we could and went to a big church.

Ben; what can I say about Ben? Ben came into my life when he was about six. We called him Benji then. Now he is Ben-jammin. We got into trouble together from the start. The first year he lived with me we got a dog and built a doghouse. When hunting season came, we snuck up and shot the neighbors pet goose by mistake. Now we go fishing.

Ben was already suffering. Ben's dad, Dave, had just recently been killed in a car accident. If you saw Dave on the street you would probably avoid him. I met him under the worst of circumstances, after hearing about him from my then current wife, his ex-wife. I was the hot shot rich guy from Alaska, come to take his wife and kid twenty-five hundred miles away. Dave lived in a run-down shingle house in a run-down neighborhood. He made me feel at home immediately. He was short, always had long hair. He was unkempt and he kept his Harley at all cost. He was one of the friendliest, easy to be with, persons I ever met. He was an ideal father; he loved his son unconditionally and painted honestly, the world for his son, as he saw it. He had a problem with drugs and alcohol that destroyed his life. He hobbled around for the last ten years of his life on legs he had destroyed in an auto accident. He died, a passenger in a friend's truck. It was a recent event. So Ben was dealing with the double whammy.

Jeremy. Jeremy became part of my extended family long before I married his mom. Jeremy and Ben. Tasha's two brothers. Jeremy is the kind of kid who takes the responsibility part of being a brother more seriously than the fun part. He and Ben became brothers from the first. Jeremy now had a little sister to boot. I can see them in the car in Fairbanks, Jeremy and Ben. Our not so sweet fourteen-year-old Tasha had found some friends and was off by herself in a car somewhere at night. Her two brothers flew like a couple of avenging angels into the teen party scene, and threatening and bullying, had tracked her down and brought her home. What else went on between these modern siblings will probably never be known to me, but I always knew that Jeremy and Ben would take care of Tasha, and they always did. When they were around. They were around now and we were here to take care of Tasha. Now they sat next to me on the edge of the end of the world. No consolation. Nothing but the depth of sadness known to the esoteric few, translatable into words by no one.

The celebration of the dead will always be a personal thing to me. The ceremony that was held that day certainly was not personal, nor was it for the family. The crowd was immense. There was a mass of flowers draped around a blown up photo of my daughter. There were candles burning in the crowd. The music was a dreary, polished dirge by an aging rock guitarist, lamenting the death of his infant son. It was manufactured, I guess, to make people feel OK about the death of a child. You know, we'll see you later on in heaven. I guarantee you, that songwriter did not write that song until some length of time after the death of his infant son. Impossible. How could he? When hurt is like an alien, breathing thing, lying festering in your chest. When the thought of heaven is buried under the trash heap of empty verse. Faith in anything was as vacuous as God's absence. Faith? Consolation? Not on this day. What is there to celebrate? There is only that an elemental change has taken place in this universe. As elemental as the movement of the tide. The tide of this universe has swept my Tasha from her place among us, off into a spiritual place of the unknown.

Spinoza is my favorite philosopher. Would it be that he was right, that heaven is nothing more than the combined consciousness of all of the departed? "The intellect of God is the sum of all mind." Is that what he meant? The mind of God is all the mentality that is scattered over space and time, the diffused consciousness that animates the world. Tasha, her grace and her beauty, the elegance she possessed in her psyche, all part of heaven? The dynamic, fundamental building blocks of heaven required that her innocence, the immaturity of her thoughts and ideas, hers and other young girls like her, must be part of what is needed to offset the cantankerous, concrete consciousness of the departed elderly, to substantiate heaven as some sort of demographic, democratic nirvana?

Who knows? But it still sucks; on this day all of it sucks. The dead? Her fate is sealed regardless of what we say or do on this day or any other from this point on. But the pain I feel on this day is not assuaged in any way by the fact that my daughter may have already enhanced the beauty of Christianity's mystical utopia. And a sentimental ballad of hope does nothing but force my cynical nature to maliciously trash the motives of the legend of rock whose soothing music now floats through this auditorium.

A fitting ceremony for my state of mind? A fitting song? On this day, the coffin would have been sitting atop a pyre of cedar. It would be covered with a cascade of Sonja roses. And the coffin would most assuredly, be closed. The funeral song? It would have been written by Neal Young, It would have been sung by Janis Joplin and Jimi Hendrix would have played guitar. A haunting, railing, demented tirade of shattered hope and bottomless pain. It would be a mournful, hateful poem written by a darkened talent, performed by a dead duet, for a departed Grace. The opening notes would be a searing riff, born skyward by bleeding fingers racked over razor sharp frets. Jimi's raging would pierce the room like the screeching of tires. Janice would scream about the terror in the heart of a fourteen-year-old girl getting thrown violently through the air…. Then silence.

It would begin again. Soft empty words, rising tensely in tortured octaves. Jimi would come in, building it. Broken dreams, vacant future, forsaken beyond. Then the two of them, this dead duet, would compete in a righteous, forlorn tirade, high, searing voice and blinding fingers. It would be a blues masterpiece. Janis would be screaming at the end, her voice flying on the wings of Jimi's scorching guitar. The guitar would then ignite, Jimi would offer his blazing guitar to the sacred pyre, as he and Janis faded into phantom light. The burgeoning blaze would enflame the room. The people there could warm their heart, cauterize their fear, or torch their grief. The Gods could then have their sacrifice to do with as they pleased.

I knew two or three kids at this school. I saw none of them. We were led to our place of honor, and we waited for Sherry, so the thing could begin. Sherry, in the sixteen years I had known her, had never been on time for anything. Today, however, I could sympathize with her tardiness. Who wouldn't want to be late to intern the spirit of your only daughter into the fabric of eternity? It was good that I was already seated when Sherry finally made her way into the gym. She came across the floor being supported on either side, by her father and boyfriend. She was in a state of complete desolation. She was just able to avoid collapse. For the first time in years, I felt emotions other than anger at the sight of her. It was an absolution for me. Years of enmity drained from me like fluid from a lanced boil. When it was gone, I felt better in a sense, but nothing remained. I felt no emotion for her at all, save a deep sympathy. Then she was seated. The show went on.

Interlude with Sherry, part three

"Who's gonna pay attention to your dreams? Who's gonna plug their ears when you scream?" The cars

You don't think that nightmares are real? You don't think that something is so bad that you lose the feeling in your legs and you can't walk? You don't think that the mind that has worked so good for you all these years can just shut down? Pain so bad that your mind tries to shut down and put a barricade between the world and your sanity. The insane, just jabbing holes at your wall made of paper, trying to get in. You feel that wall coming apart, about to shred, with any sense you have left about to fly off into the wind. A hard wind blowing through the holes in the paper wall of your sanity, trying to blow your soul out into the wind. The banshees waiting out there. Greasy, dirty Ogres waiting for you out there too. You are not gonna make it, you want some peace, your little girl is dead and there are two hundred people staring at you like you are a freak. And you don't care if you make it. Just let this be over, give me some pills and let this be over. You ever been to hell you god damn bitches out there that still got their little girls safe somewhere, not on a concrete slab somewhere? Don't look at me like that you lucky bitch. Leave me alone. God let this be over, I need some sleep.

The death of a student, and the circumstances involved, provided this particular school an opportunity to teach several abject lessons in life. In that respect, this event held a worthwhile purpose. It was a consecration of Tasha and those like her nationwide. It was a pageant of community mourning. Most of all, however, it was a warning. Any of those kids sitting in that room who thought they were immortal had better think again. Your actions can cause consequences far beyond any ability to justify them. Gratification has a price. Listen to your parents. Take responsibility for you actions. When you're gone, you are really gone. And so on. There was a genuine sadness in some of those kids. There was a brick wall there too. I commend that school for their efforts. I hated every second of it.

My beautiful niece, Rachael. She had been more part of my life than all my other nieces and nephews combined. She had been Tasha's best bud. I'm sure they had shared more than I would ever know. For the past few years, Rachael had come to visit us in the summertime when Tasha was with us. Those summers would forever be frozen in my mind. On this day, Rachael had a duty to perform. A duty of her own construction. She had to get up in front of a thousand strangers and read her poem. The poem she had written for her lost cousin.

Sister

You were very like my sister
In every single way
And I knew from the moment I met you
You would always be that way

If I had a problem
I could always come to you
And I knew your answers
Would always be helpful and true

Every time I saw you
You always made my day
And I couldn't help but wish
You were always here to stay

You always seemed to smile
Even through the toughest times
And even when you were angry
It didn't change all the while

You never turned your back on me
You never let me down
And even if I held a grudge
You always stuck around

You always seemed to comfort me
You always were so sweet
And even if your day went bad
My thoughts you'd always meet

Whenever I felt lost
You were by my side
Even through the toughest times
In you, I could confide

You always made me laugh
No matter what you said
And even if it made no sense
It could always make me smile
Everything we've ever done
Will always stay with me
And everything you've ever said
Will stay inside my memory

Every summer we've spent together
Every little trip we've made
Was something I looked forward to
Every time I thought of you

Every time you left me here
I couldn't wait till you came back
And every time you came back here
I dreaded the day you left

When I heard what happened
I couldn't believe it was true
And even though I knew it
I couldn't pull it through

Every time I think of you
Memories come and go
Happy, sad, I'm not sure
I know they'll never go

You left so many dents
When you went away
How unfair that you should leave
Without even a good-bye

I know you're up in heaven now
Looking down from above
I just hope you know
How very much you were loved

I have just one thing to say
before you turn away
I want you to remember
Of what this I will say

You are like my sister
In every single way
And I will always love
And think of you every single day

The strength of the restraining device, the device that holds heated emotions at bay, is tenuous in a direct relation to the immensity and nature of that same emotion. I don't know what it is about young girls that separates them from young boys, in the determination by people like me, that they of all things, are more fragile and therefore susceptible to greater pain than their male counterparts, particularly when I know this to be false. Still, the perception is there. Rachael on that day, in front of a thousand strangers, tested to the limit, the restraining device I just mentioned. She stood proud and strong and delivered the whole thing, uncaring what the people in that audience thought. She was there on a personal mission of love. She was uncaring, or at least not cowed, by the specter of the staged event going on around her.

The four-hour drive home offered me the opportunity to consider my young niece, Rachael. I am always amazed at the resiliency of the human heart. Is there anything more beautiful than a young woman? There are few things more difficult than to witness a grief that is so debilitating as to test the boundary of endurance. I was left to watch as grief gave depth to a young girl's beauty. It is a wonder to watch a young person when they are molting, dropping their innocence as you would shrug out of a sweater. The change is astonishing. You curse the labor involved. Becky and I had loved the times Rachael and Tasha had spent with us over the years. Watching the two of them together was like watching a bouquet bloom. I watched her now, knowing that the special relationship we had with Rachael was another casualty of this horrid event. I was powerless to do anything about it. We drove steadily south, toward the river of tears.

My sisters took care of details. Tunda, my brother, and I studied the philosophies of alcohol. Becky, Rachael and Sharon, Rachael's mother, struggled. It came time to view the body. The girls all went. Becky did not. My brother and I stayed behind. The last time I was to see my daughter was when I put her on the airplane going south back to her home. I was disgusted with myself, because I could not picture the event in my mind. My last recollections of her were phone calls and visions of her on a snowboard.

Funerals are a barbaric and Pagan event. Everybody played their part well. I forced myself to read every card that was attached to the flowers that were arranged around the funeral parlor. I was surprised at how the grapevine operated and genuinely touched by the people who had taken the time and effort to send some flowers. I was as much surprised at the people who sent flowers as those who had not. I couldn't help but think who would be there and send flowers, had it been me lying in that coffin. Vanity. I begin a journey then, down the sick mental exercise of just how badly I should be feeling as opposed to how I really felt. I didn't understand the concepts of shock or other mental defenses. I didn't know then about the process of grief and mourning. Nor did I know anything about the evil heart that beat in the chest of the Black Witch. No, not then.

I don't care to summon up the memory of the ceremony that was held that day. It was an exercise in enduring the standard remedy. It had nothing to do with the life of the young girl whose remains lay nearby. It had nothing to do with assuaging the torment of those seated there. It was the prescribed standard procedure, and so it was done. As I recall, it was a partly cloudy with a light breeze. We walked the short distance and took our places around the grave. Tasha's remains would lie for eternity within arm's length of her grandmother. This was fitting, I thought. If you looked at pictures of the two of them at age three, they looked like twins. If there is a spiritual benefit from lying close to the remains of another, then Tasha was well accompanied on her soul's journey to the Rapture. If the content of one's character is somehow mirrored by the radiance of their soul, then Tasha was living large. She was hanging with Granny. Cosmic twins.

We sat and we listened to the words. People threw their flowers onto that coffin. I watched as Tasha's mother threw her Sonja rose. It disappeared into that abyss and there was nothing left to do.

In the years since our divorce, I had avoided Tasha's mother like the plague. She had been that to me for many years; a plague. As I watched her now, I felt a true emotion for her once again. This time, sadness and pity. Whatever I was going through, I could see it all magnified on her face. I had watched our daughter emerge from Sherry's womb. She had given up of her womb. She would suffer more than I would ever know. I had grown up a lot in the time we had been split up. I now knew what was important and what was not. Being a woman, being an attractive woman in those days in Alaska was a test in and of itself. Maybe someday I could reconcile things with her.

Interlude with Sherry, part four

"Some say love, it is a razor, that leaves your soul to bleed..." Bette Midler

He was kind that day for a change. He gave me that beautiful rose. I looked at him and saw there was still something there. But who cared. I really didn't care anymore. Suki can be a real bitch, but she was the best friend I had right now and she had told me that I had to take care of Justin. That I had something to live for. That little red-headed shit. So I had a friend at least and I had the little red-headed shit that still needed me. Was that enough for me to give a damn? How was I going to get through the next few days even? Everywhere in Snohomish, people just stared at me. Even in Baring, staring people with bullshit coming out of their mouths, sad looks that meant nothing, hugs that meant nothing. I didn't have a heart anymore. The sound of it as I lay awake at night listening to it, just pissed me off. So, go to church? Why not? But what the hell good was that gonna do? Well, I had some insurance money now. What the hell was I gonna do? I had to start somewhere. My dad, the asshole had at least shown up. My brother the geek, was a good guy, my sister and me were tight. I had Benny and Justin. I had a family. Maybe it was time to try to knit them back together. At least it would give me something to do. One day to the next. Yeah, right.

There were now only two of us sitting by that hole in the ground, that fresh wound in the earth. There was nothing to be done but to leave. I got up with my Becky. We added our flowers to those that now covered the coffin. We said a few words. It was over, and not yet begun. I had gone through these last few days without seeing any light. The emotion called joy was a word on a page, three chapters gone. As we turned and started making our way to the parking lot, I looked to the distance. Cruising slowly, like a low-slung robin's egg, was an old time roadster. It stuck out like Hitler at a Bar Mitzvah. It had exactly the opposite effect on me. I felt something like the first letter of the first word of a good joke. I want to thank you Cranker, for coming that day and for bringing that car.

The party that followed was much more to my liking. I learned a lot about a lot of people that day. The attraction of people to the bereaved fell into three categories. It was broadcast from their eyes like lines on a page. What they had to say was mostly meaningless. Their eyes said it all. Some looked deep into your eyes to find a wisdom. What price are you paying? What do you know that I don't know? Some spilled sympathy from their eyes like it was a soothing potion that they were trying to pour over your hurt. And others. Well, others were glad it was you and not them. But for a day you found mostly complete honesty, at least in the eyes.

The celebration of the deceased, as it is called nowadays, ran its course. As I mentioned earlier, my family to a person, bore the brunt of the details that clutter and occlude all facets of a funeral. These people are too great in number to name here. They included all my siblings, most of their spouses and most of my nieces and nephews. Probably thirty or more. Our family is a thing of beauty, if you are willing to stretch that adjective to its abstract limits. There are ten of us, the youngest born in 1956. Through these forty-five years, we have been able to maintain a common purpose. That purpose, as conceived and spun to life by Granny, is to always stay close and to help each other out. As of this writing, each and every one of us has worked to maintain that goal. The continuing endurance of this most basic form of human companionship has survived by the persistent resolve of each individual. Everyone who has lived forty some years in this country knows how difficult that can be. Age differences, spouses and philosophical differences have tested this remarkable longevity. This bond has been bent a few times but never broken. I believe this relationship will last until the final member of this family unit is planted into the embrace of the black mother, Mother Earth. This bond that I share with my family has always been the basis of my social conscience.

I suppose that I am an anomaly in these times of ours. I harbor a deep distrust of portions of the medical profession and virtually that entire branch of medicine that deals with psychiatry. I suppose most of this comes from the fact that my mom was a cynic when it came to doctors. She had a firm belief that if you ate right and stayed in reasonable physical shape, that you had a good chance of good health and long life. She told me at one particular time in her life that she might have been insane for a while. I firmly believe that she was simply dealing with the Black Witch at that time. Still, she obstinately avoided shrinks. She also harbored a bias of experts. Most of the experts in her life were diploma-ordained experts, college graduates who were to become her bosses at her Head Start job. Inevitably, she would have to lead these "experts" around until they learned the ropes. I guess the Head Start program is a stepping-stone for bureaucrats in Social Services. Maybe here is where I got part of my bias against the educational institutions of higher learning. She hated the pill mentality of a lot of her friends and always cautioned me against taking medication when I didn't have to. She had a distrust of people who might perpetuate any condition for their own benefit. People of her generation seemed to be more self-reliant and definitely more reticent. The thought of airing your dirty laundry to anyone was repellent to her.

The idea of seeing a shrink to tell your innermost thoughts, your fears, your desires, is simply not acceptable to me. The current practice is to employ a counselor for every occasion. If I can't solve a problem by analyzing it, discussing it with friends and family, I usually rationalize it away. It's not for everybody and maybe it's the root of a lot of my problems. Be that as it may. Becky is of similar thoughts I think, possibly with the exception of the clergy. She might have been able to rid herself of these black years earlier had she chosen to seek some guidance. Then again, she was always worried about the money. We had no insurance at the time. Becky has a tremendous amount of willpower. She quit smoking one day after twenty some years and that was it. But she beat this depression on her own. I certainly never made it easy on her.

In those days of grim reality, I didn't reach out for professional help of any kind. I reached no further than my friends and family. I made it through that initial ordeal, just by going home. I cannot begin to imagine living through the drudgery of those days had not most of my responsibilities been deflected to my family. However, the door swings both ways.

I was sitting talking to one of my brothers when Kim, my sister-in-law, walked over to me and firmly insisted that I had to talk to Rachael. Now! I followed Kim to Rachael's room. Rachael was sitting on the floor crying. She was surrounded by her female cousins. On her lap were all the letters that Tasha had sent to her over the years. Scattered around the room were pictures of Tasha, her and Tasha. When she saw me, Rachael covered her face with her hands and she sobbed. Her cousins sat in a protective semi-circle looking bewildered. The air in that room was humid with tears. What was the impetus for this particular stage of desolation? Closure.

Closure. The psychological poster child who is trotted out to poultice the tragedy out of modern day mayhem. Closure. The girls had all felt it was necessary to view Tasha's body. Rachael was now tormented by the inadequacies of the embalmers. She dropped her hands and demanded to know why the body didn't look like Tasha. Four sets of young female eyes turned to me for answers. Me, who had no answers.

Two days earlier, I had sat in awe. Rachael had always been my *little* niece. Then at a time in her life when she should have been stressing about learning to drive, boys and what to wear to the prom, life had come crashing down on her, bearing with it, unfathomable pain. Rachael had succeeded in casting the horrendous nature of Tasha's death into a mental compartment and sealed it there. She had borne the incomprehensibility of seeing her cousin lose at the infinitesimal odds of Russian Roulette being played by young people daily on our nation's roadways. She had taken her first steps as a young woman. She had begun dealing with this, her first tragedy. She had tucked her childhood neatly away to honor her cousin. She had stood up in front of a huge room full of strangers and given her personal eulogy to her beloved cousin. Then after all that, she had been blindsided by the sight of a lifeless form that lay tucked in the soft satin folds of eternity. The sight of her cousin lying in a coffin, looking like a porcelain caricature was simply a lie too great to bear.

What do you say when a broken-hearted girl of sixteen stares at you in utter desolation and says, "That wasn't Tasha in that coffin, it didn't look anything like her. That *was not Tasha.*" Closure. Rachael's eyes were beseeching me for answers. Me, who had no answers. "Of course it didn't look like Tasha." I said "You see Rach, Tasha had a Spirit. Tasha was laughs, she was smiles, smirks and hugs. Tasha's spirit was the sum total that was her mind. She was sadness and she was joy. She was songs and she was poems. Her spirit came from a place within her soul and shined out her eyes. Her spirit poured from her in her dreams and her smiles. Her spirit shaped the curve of her mouth, the light of her eyes. When Tasha died, when her spirit escaped from the vessel of her body, it left an empty shell. What you saw was that shell, where her spirit had lived. With Tasha gone, that shell is now empty. Tasha was not an empty shell, so how could that shell you saw possibly resemble Tasha at all?" or some such words. I left those girls to hug each other in solace and went searching for some of my own.

Sometime in the days that followed, Becky and I were at my brother, Brad's house. At some point, Brad and Kim sat me down. It seemed that they had taped some news footage of the accident that had taken my daughter's life. Did I want to see it? How could I not? The film was typical of a local news broadcast. The unseen reporter narrated the known circumstances. Four teenagers had snuck out late at night. The oldest, a boy of sixteen, had "borrowed" his dad's car, of course unknown to both parents. Two young boys, two young girls. A scenario replayed countless times every day in this country. The four kids had gone for a ride. They had taken turns driving. The curve had come up very fast. Both girls were ejected. One was critically injured. The other, my daughter Natasha Lynn Scott, had suffered severe trauma to the head and died instantly. Both boys suffered minor injuries. No seatbelts had been worn. No evidence of drugs or alcohol. The footage accompanying this narrative was the standard emergency vehicles, lights flashing, police standing around. Then a shot of a covered body being wheeled on a gurney and moved into the ambulance. The narrator finished with some statistics. There you have it. Just another day in the city.

What I am about to say is bound to infuriate some of the parents out there. I take responsibility for that. I love the fact that my daughter snuck out of windows at night. It was what her mom did. It was what her step-mom did. It is what her father did. I wish someone else would have been killed. I wish that particular lottery had a different winner. I wish she had snuck out on some other night, when she was a little older. Every person of my generation whom I call a friend, did exactly what

Tasha did that night at one time or another in their lives. The problem is that kids mature earlier in these times of ours, and the times are more dangerous. When we did it, we were seventeen, not fifteen. When we did it, there weren't things like crack, date rape drugs, AIDS, drive-by shootings, etc. We did our sneaking in a world that was not rife with danger. In those days it was just the common sort of trouble; young kids doing stupid things in a time of relative innocence. Every girl I have ever had any interest in would sneak out windows. They were the ones who were excited by the adventure. The ones who would always test authority. The ones who would dine and dash. The ones who tested the patience of their parents. But none of them had died.

Chapter IV
THE BLACK DAYS

"There's someone in my head, but it's not me." Pink Floyd

Some days later, we left the spring behind and went home to Alaska. Becky had a week before she had to go back to Columbus to finish her training. It became official one blustery morning. I found the morning paper open on the breakfast bar and Becky nowhere in sight. Dumbfounded, I read my daughter's obituary. Then I had to go find Becky. I would learn over and over again in the coming months about the weapons at the disposal of the Black Witch. This surprise attack was not her most formidable strike. At the time, it seemed her most hideous.

I took Becky to the airport early one morning the following week. I came home to the empty house. At the top of the stairs, mounted on the wall so as not to be missed, was the one family portrait we had taken. Tasha was sitting between her brothers. She was about fourteen at the time. I glanced away and headed for the kitchen for a cup of coffee. I got a beer out instead and sat down at the table. And so, as she sat leering opposite, I began my formal engagement with the Black Witch.

I stared into her vapid, merciless eyes as the beer cans multiplied on the table in front of me. Our breakfast ritual would continue over the next several months whenever Becky was out of town. Our little ground handling company was stagnant. I was fortunate to have the employees that I did. They had names like Ugalino, Diaz, Tes and Tufaga. Thanks to these people and our two supervisors, Wolfman and Stan, the place pretty well ran itself. That left time for me to dwell. Maybe that is the power of the Black Witch. The inclination to dwell. The necessity to dwell. The lack of a defense to combat the necessity to dwell.

My days became monotonous in their replication. Breakfast beer with the Black Witch. Afternoons rummaging through paperwork at our office. My sole responsibility, at least the most important, was to procure some new contracts for our small company. At this project, I was a total failure. Our company was simply too small. We had only enough equipment to service our current contracts. We couldn't afford to buy more equipment without a new contract, and couldn't get new contracts without more equipment. I made pointless phone calls to indifferent middle managers. The decision-makers were in Reno, Los Angeles, Dallas or Honolulu. I faxed endless proposals and the day would pass. Then, I would stop at Value Liquor on the way home, make sure I had enough beer for that night and just a little more, just in case. Then I would go home. Home to dwell.

Trash on TV. My previous brushes with the law kept me home where I drank alone. The sit and dwell syndrome slowly revealed my personal definition of depression. Lack of joy. Gray skies and lack of joy. Morning beers with the witch. So now, lack of joy and just a dash of paranoia. Anyone who has stared down the barrel of financial failure can understand part of my dilemma. It's like you're traveling down a long hallway lined with doors on either side. The end of the hallway is a large mirror. Every door on either side is a way out. All these doors have combination locks. They are all locked. You keep trying all the combinations you can think of, but none of them will open even one of the damned doors. So finally you must face the mirror. In it you see gray hair, wrinkles and fear in the eyes. You turn around and start a determined march back down the hall to the mirror at the other end. Each trip takes about a year. All the way down the hall you think about the platitudes.

Perseverance, cream rising to the top, time heals all wounds, part of the thirty-fourth Psalm. My test for relevance has always been results. So right away, I discard any religious liniments. It would be high hypocrisy for me to seek any spiritual remedies. And I knew that. So now you are faced with the stark reality of purely atheist, or at least agnostic thought. There is a rational way out of this mess. There surely is, but that will only chop off one horn of the dilemma. How do you reconcile yourself to the arbitrary nature of your mortality, your posterity? Is it even important? Your sole biological offspring has been terminated. You have had a vasectomy. Is that important? Immediately, two distinct and dissimilar images spring into your mind. You are forced to deal with your own shallow platitudes.

One image is that of a beautiful girl I met once years ago. She was a blackjack dealer at a casino in the resort at Victoria Falls, Zambia. The nametag she wore on the crisp white shirt has faded from memory. Her Aussie accent still rings across the years. She had that remarkable beauty seen so infrequently. Startlingly beautiful. She wore her looks almost sheepishly. A gentle warmth reigned in her smile. Where so often you see the haughty arrogance of the strikingly beautiful, her eyes shone with a friendly innocence. I was twenty-four years old. During the past year I had been surrounded by books and a pilot or two who had revealed truths about the world, politics and social conscience.

Armed with these platitudes and the infallibility of newfound truths that only the very young can be so certain of, I set to work displaying my sophistication and intellect. It was 1974. Vietnam, Cold War, Apartheid, Oil Crises. Most of all though, the invincibility of my own empirical wisdom. I was twenty-four years old. All this girl wanted out of life was babies. A good home, a fine man and babies. With the aid of my intrepid pilot buddy, we ripped her world to shreds. How could she think of bringing babies into a world teetering on the edge of imminent destruction? There was upheaval and insurrection at every quarter. Better to take the booze cruise, live for the here and now and accept the inevitability of mankind as the great destroyer.

The girl withstood the barrage of hubris in good humor for a time. She understood the nature of all assault. She knew our real motives. But we were ruthless. The onslaught continued. In good order she was reduced to tears. She flung the deck of cards at us and retreated, sobbing. The next dealer cheated us so blatantly that we finally called him on it. We were invited to leave. The Ugly Americans. The platitudes I championed that day? The arbitrary nature of the Universe. The absence of God. The insanity of man. The moral injustice of bringing a child into the whole mess. Now, a quarter century later, I had chosen to ignore all the rubbish that those same platitudes had come to represent. So how, at this juncture, was I going to handle the arbitrary nature of the Universe that had just struck down my beautiful baby girl?

The second image was that of my mother, when she had found out that I was going to have a vasectomy. She was upset. She wanted me to understand the finality of the act. Here my social conscience platitude had come into play. I had one child. I had a stepson. The earth in the balance and all that crap. I was sure in my decision, pompous almost. Of course I did the deed. And of course, my mom was more right than I was. In the days after Tasha's death, it was a common topic between the Black Witch and me, and only the Witch knew what I could never tell anyone else.

Religion is a crutch. The universe is chaos and random disorder. This blackness you feel is physical in nature. The life of your recently deceased daughter is now meaningless. It was time to live my convictions. The flame of my daughter's existence was extinguished. Memories were valid only as a learning tool. Everything was in the here and now. So, deal with it. The arrogance of the atheist. The price of the atheist. My daughter lay in a black hole in the earth. That certainly was a reality. Now the normal sequence of birth and death had been turned upside down. Mourning for your mother was a natural consequence of your respective ages. Watching a withered and tired body fade slowly was heartrending, but it was natural. But now you have to deal with the child that was, and suddenly was no more. And you begin to understand how much of your life was connected to the welfare of hers. And then you have to face the first of many other black truths. Personal failures as a parent. I was waiting for her to grow up before I got to know her, and her, me. I took the time to call her but infrequently, for you see, I, me, asshole, doesn't like to talk on the phone. You want to search the pasture high and low for bullshit? That one's right outside the barn door. I would call her every two weeks or so. She would call me more often. The two or three weeks in the summer were really the only time we spent together. And those were fun times. The last eight years of her life, it was mainly the summers. I didn't have to deal with the schoolwork, the sad times, the illnesses. I never really got to hear about her problems and dreams. I knew hardly anything about her normal routine. I was almost completely ignorant of my daughter's life. I was waiting for her to grow up. We would have such great times and talks, after she grew up. Tasha lived for almost sixteen years. The greater part of eleven of those years, we spent apart. I didn't even know my own daughter. I was mostly caught up in my own personal troubles. The "Woe is me" syndrome Sherry aptly called it. Now, my identity rests for eternity in the scant few years remaining to me. What is the use in, or point of that? And the Black Witch laughed when she threw it in my face. "Your daughter is dead and you are sitting here feeling sorry for...you. You pathetic soulless bastard. She lies in a black hole of your atheist creation and you moan about yourself. You deserve to be a soulless bastard, and all you deserve is my company." Then there was the damn tape. The damn tape plays over and over again in your head. "Died instantly." What were her last thoughts? What did she really think of me? What terrors did she suffer that morning in that instant? What? What? What?

Then you begin the endless attempts to retrieve those memories. You practice over and over. You need to picture her face, to remember her voice. You take your can of beer and go stare into the mirror. After only a few days, you can't do it. You can't do it. No you can't, but ah, the Witch.

You sit bolt upright in bed. Your heart is racing, you're scared shitless. The Witch laughs. A terrible dream. Tasha, plain as day, her eyes flashing, and she is really pissed off at me. It's such a terrible dream. And then the feeling of dread. It's three AM sometime in your forty-eighth year when you learn the true meaning of dread. I can see her face fine in the black of the room, I can hear her voice, but now I don't want to, not like that.

Interlude with Sherry, part five

"Well she's gone to meet her maker, back to where she came from, come to save her soul..." "Angel" by The Eurythmics

I had the best dream last night. Tasha plain as day. She was smiling, her eyes were shining and she was so happy. "Mom, I made it into the book. I made it mom. You're gonna make it too mom." She had gone on and told me how everything was going to be alright, she was going to be fine and I was going to be fine, she never mentioned her dad, not once. I had some really good days after that. I had decided I was going to get out of Baring and go somewhere where the sun shined more. I was so tired of the rain and the snow. I didn't really care about the mountain, snowboarding, all of that. It all reminded me of her and how much I missed her and everybody said get over it. Even Benny, get over it. Get over it, how stupid is that? A hole in your heart, a piece of your brain that is all Tasha, the memories. I actually saw her in the dream. So I see Abbey and I get pissed off at Suki, how crazy is that? At least I'm off the pills and not drinking so much. Got to get out of Baring though and find the sun. That will make it better. That'll help.

Then you come upon something in the Bible. *Proverbs Chapter 1, 23:31, "Turn you at* my reproof: behold, I will pour out my spirit unto you, I will make known my words unto you. Because I have called, and ye refused; I have stretched out my hand and no man regarded; but ye have set at naught all my counsel and would have none of my reproof; I also will laugh at your calamity; I will mock when your fear cometh; When your fear cometh as desolation, and your destruction cometh as a whirlwind; when distress and anguish cometh upon you. Then shall they call upon me, but I will not answer; they shall seek me early but they shall not find me: For that they hated knowledge, and did not choose the fear of the Lord: They would none of my counsel: they despised all my reproof. Therefore shall they eat of the fruit of their own way, and be filled with their own devices." Well there is was. If there was anything to the truth in the Bible then it was all laid out for me.

Platitudes, No one ever says "It wasn't your fault." Really. Well just why was Tasha living in a different house than me? Would it have been any different had I been there? Probably not. Probably not? Remember, the universe is a series of purely arbitrary events that no one can control. One life smashes into another. Sometimes joy, sometimes carnage. The camera slowly recedes to show countless people smashing their lives into other lives. The images get smaller and smaller, and then you see the earth as it hurtles through space and disappears into the blackness. Then the sun slowly recedes to a point of one light among billions of others. The purely chaotic Universe. Given the facts and the state of my mind, what is the point? Getting old sure ain't as fun as being young. Poor sucks compared to not poor. Then you get a summons from your asshole ex-partner. Cool. Now you get to deal with some asshole lawyer. Make that two asshole lawyers; one for him one for you. And that Black evil Witch just laughs. "Woe is you. Poor Steve. Your daughter has maggots in her eyes, is that why you're crying?"

Platitudes. Self Esteem. Now here is a hot topic. They talk about it on the TV, in classrooms and especially at rehab, or so I am told. How important is that. Not very, at least not on The Jerry Springer show. How well do we like our self today? Me? Well let's see. I'm broke, had to borrow money for the funeral. My old partner won the lawsuit; there goes my last asset. It was only psychological anyway. My daughter rages at me in dreams. Mr. Big Shot is getting creamed at every turn. Counseling? Costs money; besides I'm smarter than they are anyway.

My only solace, breakfast with the Black Witch. But then my real solace arrives. Becky is back home. She banishes the Witch from the house along with the breakfast beers. And spring has come.

Spring has come. Becky is a checked-out Hercules flight attendant. One of only eight in the world. The company we both work for, Southern Air Transport, is flying passengers and cargo in a configuration called a combi. If you want to lighten your mood on a spring day, just go for an airplane ride with Captain Broughton, your old lady, fifteen miners and land at a gold mine on top of a mountain. Right on! Nixon Forks is a gold mine on top of a mountain in the wilds of Alaska. The runway is about a mile long, made of gravel, slightly slanted. The Lockheed Hercules is the world's largest bush airplane.

To get to Nixon Forks, you fly northwest from Anchorage for about an hour. In a line of rolling hills off in the distance, you see one hill that has a rust-colored gash carved out of the summit. You circle over the runway to announce your arrival, line up and touch down at about one hundred and ten knots. The runway is wide enough so the wings have some clearance. You've got ridges on both sides. As soon as you touch down, Captain Broughton puts all four engines into full reverse and gets hard on the brakes at the same time. The ridges are flying by off your wingtips, ahead you are hell-bent for leather, heading straight on into a cut bank some sixty feet high. You finally stop in a swirl of noise and dust, and depending on how the landing went, you might be staring into the face of that cut bank. A really cool rush and everybody onboard loves it. You unload your freight of humanity and supplies and load up more humanity and gold ore. Then you blast off. You spin around in the face of the cut bank and go flat out down the runway. When the airplane rotates into the air, it's like launching off the deck of an aircraft carrier because you are immediately out over a valley that falls off the mountainside. This kind of flying is just cool. For a couple of hours at least, your demons are held at bay, the Black Witch is just a mote in your mind's eye.

But this, even this, in now in jeopardy. A new company is coming into the market. This new airline has the same Hercules aircraft. They are an Alaskan company. This fact is a political advantage. The parent company is a large and successful transportation company. Both my job, Becky's job and the main profit center of our little ground handling company are now at risk.

Becky is gone again.

Southern Air Transport has a military contract for the Air Force, with an airplane based in Europe. Becky has never traveled, so is excited about the opportunity to go to Europe and get paid. The Witch is back. My days with the Black Witch were almost a discipline. Wake up to a hangover and remorse. You promised yourself that today would be different. But it wasn't. She was at first seductive. "Go on, have just one beer, just to take the edge off." After the third beer she became your friend. "You and me baby. No one else understands or cares. Only me and you baby." She'd send me out to take care of whatever business was really pressing, always with the promise of a beer later on. Payroll, but not enough money. Rent that's a month behind. The guys need kneepads and flashlights. The company plugged along, always spending next week's check, today. A tap dance and an understanding banker. But then it was home to the Black Bitch, the mistress.

And could she drink. She would match you beer for beer, until as regular as clockwork, come on, just one little pull. So it would be one little pull on a half-pint of Jim beam, maybe two. Then it was one AM and she would entice me off to bed with the promise of sleep. Sometimes it was an empty promise. Sometimes the promise was kept. Which was worse, depended on any dreams. I had only one really loathsome dream in those first few months. It turned out that my dead daughter hated me. The Witch descended into the dark recesses of my worst fears. She looked around in there and pulled a beauty out of those cobwebs. The Black Witch became Tasha. She knew more about me than anyone could. As real as a bleeding wrist, she looked as pretty as a rose. The filth that spewed from her gentle smile crucified my confidence, left me hanging on the pale light of a winter morning in the general gloom of that closed-in bedroom. The feeling in my chest was a brand new experience. I was forty-eight and my reasoning was at the elementary level. I had no rational way to deal with the experience. I simply had to bear it. The emotion was one of fear mixed with an unreasonable sense of guilt. I had an anxiety that made my head shake by simply having to look into the eyes of another human being. I was afraid of sleep for the next couple of nights. My daughter hated me from beyond. Whether it was true or not had no impact. That night in that dream, she had loathed me. The dream, like a come-on from a con man, had the power to rob me. I knew the deck might be stacked, but could I resist the temptation to cut those cards and see if I got lucky? Rob me of what? Outside of my wife, the only good thing I had left to me was self-respect and hope for the future. The residue of that dream remains with me today. The dream has not returned.

The nature of the Black Witch is that she preys on your confidence and feeds on your esteem. It is not a sustained attack. When Becky was home, the Witch might leave. She took most of the booze with her. Spring was coming. The simple appearance of a sunny day would be enough. Becky and I would go for a drive or just look at the mountains through our front window. No Witch in sight. But she always came back. Constant reminders in those first days. A box of Tasha's things arrived in the mail one day. A touch of empathy from her mother. A return of the Witch for me. Women operate on a mystical plane where emotions are able to embody the objects of those who have owned those objects. A woman can pick up an old Easter dress, hold it to her and feel the presence of a six-year-old girl. Like the thread of Tasha's spirit was interwoven among the cloth. I am unable to make that connection. Becky looked through the box. In another room, I drank a beer. Becky caressed the chain of a pendant. I had a pull from my old buddy, Beam. The Black Witch winked and I thought of those hours after one AM. I guessed at all this. I've never had the courage to look in that box. I don't want to know what's in there. (Years later I looked in that box and among other things, I found the poem written by my niece Rachael, quoted earlier)

The sun stayed longer and longer every day. June is one long day in the northern latitudes. If you are robbed of your sleep, you don't notice so much. The sun is a tonic that provides a constant flow of energy. People had stayed away for some months. But now my buddy, Bill, was coming to Anchorage. I had known Bill from almost my first days in Alaska. Bill is a bull of a man. His attitudes are huge, his appetites are huge and his heart is huge.

Bill Largen has been a friend of mine since I met him some 25 years ago in a small town in darkest Africa, Lobatse, Botswana. He was a character in that part of my life that I now consider the golden age. It was a time when all things were possible, extraordinary events were commonplace. The people I worked with were almost family, and careless abandon took a close second place to work ethic. The events surrounding our first meeting set a tone for our relationship that was destined to be a roller coaster ride that was a lot more than an empty analogy.

The next two years, I would share a lot of experiences with Billy. He came to be a close friend. We were destined to travel three continents together. We shared a lot. We drank together. We played cards together. He beat me seventeen straight times at cribbage once, a thing he never let me forget. We both got shot at and we both fell in love, many times.

Bill got reacquainted with Jesus after he returned from Africa. It never changed our friendship. It changed his life, and maybe not for the better. Bill had absolute faith in his Savior and the commandments that structured his life. Bill was Catholic. Bill still had his huge appetites. Bill met a woman who was both beautiful and wild. He married her. He had two girls of his own and adopted another, who was the child of his wife. The times faded the beauty of his wife, but did nothing to stem her wild nature. She was as a-Christian as Bill was ardent. But she was Bill's wife in the eyes of the Lord, and that was the final word. The fifteen years or so that he was married to her might have tested the patience of Job. Bill however, was another matter. He was married to her until the end, period.

Bill was the hardest working person I have ever met. Bill always had his real job, the one he did mostly at night, and his other job, the one they paid him for, during the day. Fairbanks, during the last fifteen years of the past century was a trial for a lot of folks. The economy had been ravaged in the mid-eighties with the plunge in oil prices. Bill simply got more jobs and managed to do OK. I made a point to see him as often as I could. He had the personality that was ebullient, I suppose. He was either telling a joke or laughing. He and Becky got along grandly. He had given up trying to save my soul, but Becky's was another matter. Bill was coming to Anchorage for a couple of days. He worked part-time for my little company. We had an aircraft de-icer that was particularity temperamental. Bill would come to town a couple of times a year. When he came to Anchorage, he would stay at our house and he would work on the de-icer.

Bill showed up in the late afternoon. The Witch was banished when Bill arrived. No matter what the circumstances surrounding, the room that occupied Bill was one of joy and laughter. "Are we having fun yet?" He walked through the door with a smile as big as Texas. We spent the evening talking about old times. We generally avoided talk of the present. Bill was a partner in a soil remediation company. The company had been struggling for some time. Bill had every dollar he possessed invested in the company and some more money he didn't have. It had been a constant struggle with partners and ex-partners for the better part of three years. I could identify completely. So we talked of old times.

Becky, who now had some flying stories of her own, told Bill he would now have to listen to her war stories. For the past several years, whenever Bill came to visit, Becky would have to sit and listen to Bill and me rehash all our stories about our days overseas. Particularly about the time we had spent in Africa. It had been a wonderful time for both of us. It was a time that held a special meaning for us, but poor Becky had to sit and listen to the rehashing. When Becky and Bill were alone, he would start on Becky. Bill just naturally assumed the role of big brother to her. Bill had not had a drink since he became re-aquatinted with his personal savior. He knew it to be the best road for him to follow. He naturally assumed it was his duty to try and put Becky on that road. That, and of course, Bill always wanted me to find The Way. He used Becky as a tool to that end. Becky is a naturally spiritual person. Those times with Bill always made her happy. The two of them would roar with laughter for hours on end. It was a joy to have Bill around during those dark days. Bill never said much to me about the death of my daughter. He and Becky talked about it a lot.

It was the middle of June. My daughter had been born in June, almost sixteen years ago to the day. Bill knew that. Becky had told him. So, Bill tried to take the pall out of the occasion. Bill had once beaten me seventeen times in a row at cribbage. He never let me forget the fact. On this night we played cribbage. I can't tell you who won; I don't remember. But we passed the night in good company. All three of us having a good time. When it was over, Bill arranged to meet me in the afternoon of the next day. He had business to attend to in the morning. He always greeted us with the "Are we having fun yet?" That night he went downstairs, leaving us with that same salutation.

The next morning, Becky greeted Bill with a big breakfast. Bill is the same age as I am. His artificial ankles have forced him to hobble around for the past twenty years. They could slow him, but certainly not stop him. But he had become somewhat overweight. He came up the stairs short of breath, but laughed it off. We had our usual banter over breakfast, and Bill, always in a hurry, was on his way. After he left, Becky mentioned something about his shortness of breath. Becky had just been through training as a flight attendant. Part of that training involves recognizing potential health problems in passengers. She mentioned that maybe Bill ought to see a doctor. My response was, "Bill's a big boy. It's his body and I can't tell him anything anyway."

I met Bill in the afternoon. It was a sunny, warm day. He intended to spend the rest of the day at my company's small warehouse/office. I was involved with paperwork of one kind or another. After spending a few minutes with Bill, badmouthing our partners, I left him just outside the open warehouse door. He had set up a small table there so he could work outside. He had one of the deicer's furnaces torn apart and was cleaning it. Bill and I were alone that day.

I could only spend so much time in the office. I was not cut out for that kind of work. I walked back to see how Bill was doing. I went through the open warehouse door. Bill was standing at the table, kind of leaning on it. I asked him if he was OK. "Life in the sub-arctic is for young guys," he said "This getting old, sucks." I watched him for a minute. He went back to what he was doing. I walked away. I made it halfway across the warehouse when I heard the part he was working on fall to the cement. Then I heard a sound that stopped my heart. It was kind of like a cement bag falling. I called out his name and nothing, no response. I ran out the warehouse door. Bill was lying on his side, his chest heaving. I bent over him, "Bill, Bill." His eyes were kind of flickering. "Bill, Bill." His breaths were coming in great gasps. The nearest phone was sixty feet away. I ran, dialed 911. The attendant answered on the first ring. I told her what had happened, told her I thought it was a heart attack. She got all the necessary information. My name, location, etc. She then told me to roll him on his back, clear his tongue and give him three breaths of mouth-to-mouth, Then place my hands just below his sternum and apply pressure three times to that area. Repeat this procedure three times, then return.

When I got back to Bill he wasn't breathing. I did as the 911 person had told me. I looked around for help, but there was none. I couldn't help thinking what Bill was going to say later about me giving him a full lip-lock, not once but three times. Lip-lock, that's what Bill had always called a kiss. I then ran back to the phone. The person asked me how it was going. I told her. She said just to keep doing what I was doing until the ambulance showed up. When I got back to Bill, the color was fading, he seemed to have lost twenty pounds and he seemed small and withered. He looked bad. I kept up the routine. I could see the main road from where I sat straddled over Bill. I heard the ambulance coming, and then I watched it go by, lights flashing. Shit! I knew seconds were vital. I didn't know if I should keep up with the CPR or run into the street. I waited perhaps thirty seconds, keeping up my routine. When I saw a car pull up in the front parking lot, I took off. I ran up to the car door and told the startled man to drive as fast as he could, run down the goddamned ambulance and bring it back here. Then I ran back to Bill. I was in the middle of the mouth-to-mouth when the ambulance came around the corner. In seconds, four people took my place. One was left to gently push me away and take a good look at me.

It was not going well and I knew it. Within a matter of a minute or so, they had the cardiac phones out. They gave him at least two jolts. I watched his body jump slightly as they fired electricity into his heart. All the while, they were rolling him onto a stretcher. His body, I knew it well enough, his body had turned that deathly gray color I had seen on a recent occasion. I knew. The paramedic knew. We all knew. The paramedic who had been assigned to me assured me that it wasn't over. I nodded. By now a small crowd had gathered. Where the hell had they all been fifteen minutes ago? The ambulance was pulling up to the main road. It turned left and was gone. The paramedic was still looking into my eyes. "You all right?" he kept staring at my eyes. "You did a good job, the best you could. Nothing more you could have done." He assured me that once they got Bill to the hospital he had a chance. Bill would have said "Right, about as much chance as a snowball in hell." The paramedic left. I stared at the crowd until they all went away. I went inside to my partner's desk. He always kept a bottle of whiskey there. I took a good long pull. I started making phone calls, Becky first.

Bernie, my partner in Fairbanks took care of all the dirty work. He called the wife and mother. They would soon be on the way. The Black Witch is a dirty little wench who has the power to envelop your heart in a viscous, palpable dread. She can stuff your head with images of desolation. She can perch undetected on the shelf of your inner ear and offer plausible solutions. At times, she is truly your friend. And that is the essence of her power. The power to plunge you up to your neck in doom and throw you a life-ring. But sometimes, temporary solutions are what are desperately needed to see the sun rise again. It's all about the sun. Tomorrow can damn sure not be worse than today. So you grab that life ring.

I locked the office. I had no need or no desire to go to the hospital. Billy was dead. Tomorrow would be soon enough. I stopped at Value Liquor. I got a fifth of Jack Daniels and a beer to go. I drank the beer on the two miles it took to get to my place. I walked up the stairs, no avoiding that. Tasha smiled at me from the wall at the top. I walked to the counter that divides the kitchen from the living room and pulled up a barstool. I set old Gentlemen Jack on the counter. Becky appeared. She had been crying. She spoke the words she had to say and then became silent, her eyes resting on the bottle. She walked into the kitchen and took down a water glass. Hard drinkers from an earlier time would have said that she poured me four fingers. She took the bottle and poured the rest down into the sink. I had the Black Witch, but I had Becky as well.

I sipped at the Jack until I stared at an empty glass. I wanted more. Becky shook her head. Becky went into the bedroom to cry, she knew what I was thinking and she was thinking the same thing. I looked beyond where the bottle had recently sat, so full of promise. The calendar told the whole story, June fifteenth. Father's Day. It would have been my daughter's sixteenth birthday. It certainly was a day to remember.

I once had read a newspaper article where the word "memoryscape" was given life. An Alaskan native was talking about his "memoryscapes." Each period in your life is like a mosaic made up of people and events. The mosaic that contained my life overseas was a particularly lavish one. It was full of exotic locals, peoples from hundreds of lands and the vigor and recklessness of youth. Now when I put that slide on the screen of my memory, it's shot full of holes. I think I know what Dennis Hopper feels like when he sees a rerun of "Rebel without a Cause." Imagine him watching that movie, and one by one, the characters played by now dead actors fade and disappear, swept away by the currents of time. James Dean, Natalie Wood, Nick Adams, Sal Mineo, Rochelle Hudson, William Hopper, Jim Backus, Ann Doran. All gone.

The word "friend" is bandied about almost to the point of meaninglessness. But to two people who take that word to heart, the meaning is clear and never needs to be spoken. To lose a friend is to lose part of your identity. So many times in your life you have an experience that is noteworthy, unique, or maybe just hilarious. When there is someone there to share that experience, it lends dimension to it. Over years you can laugh about those things, what Billy called war stories. Now, somehow, those times lose …luster at least; that sense of animation where your past is like a cartoon in your mind... certainly value. Those parts of your life are forever changed. The magic is taken from those times because part of the essence of the event, a character who shared the stage, is no more. Where before, the event had a real life in the consciousness minds of at least two people, now, that has been cut in half. Your life has lost a measure of validation.

In one of his books, John McDonald offers up an analogy that touches a chord in this melody. I bend it here a little. It goes something like, when you reach that time in your life when you are on your own, you wade into a stream. The stream is full of people of all ages. In that steam you choose a spot where those people you value are all around you. Other people wade in as time goes by. The number of people increases, to a point. But, through time, you get weary or sick, and one by one you watch as the people who you value, those people around you weaken and are swept away. These losses, along with the price of aging, simply make you more aware of the current, which is moving at the same pace as always, but the perception that it has grown stronger is real. I had lived my whole life and no one had yet been swept away. In a space of a little over a year, I had watched three people who were very important to me, move past me, downstream, gone. It seemed that the current was picking up. The will to live has a lot to do with the quality of life. The quality of life has a lot to do with the company you are able to keep.

I have often wondered about clinical conditions like shock. I wondered if you could suffer something like that in degrees over a period of time. I will never know about that. Doctors and medical people in general often tell you what they think is best, rather than the truth. There are many psychological terms that I have heard with derision over the years. Words like "closure" and "post-traumatic." I am a fatalist at heart. A fatalist and a realist. Get over it. Don't wallow in it, get over it. But the Black Witch loves to wallow. The longer, the better. She loves to stand towering over you as you sit with tears running down your face in a darkened room. That is the height of her power, the height of her pleasure. Try as I might, the Black Witch had her way with me on occasion. It was a concession on my part. But my only concession. I tried to pick my spots, but usually, they picked me. Mostly it was songs. I hardly ever listen to the radio at home. So on the road, by myself usually, it would be one of two songs that got me. Whenever those songs came on the radio I was helpless and I would have to pull over and cry like a baby. This went on for months. I got fed up. I decided to battle the Black Witch. I would have been a lot better off if I had chosen to eradicate her.

There is only one way to battle the Black Witch. You can only battle her on her terms. She has every advantage. The whole battle goes on inside your head. You have to operate under the rules of convention. She has no such restraints. So when you are tired because you haven't slept more than two hours a night for a week or so, not her problem. So, the company you work for is going broke. So what, there's a beer in the refrigerator. Lack of sleep is the Witch's most potent weapon. There is simply no defense against it. The root of most delusions for normal people is lack of sleep. You combine lack of sleep with a steady ration of alcohol for a couple of weeks, fantastic things happen. And they are all bad, and you don't believe them, but you give them credence. You know, nah that's impossible -- well maybe. But the thought doesn't go away. It lies next to you all night long. It's like steam in a cooking pot. You can't see it, but lift the lid and it comes billowing out and burns your hand.

I had planned to go south to Portland. My brother had an annual golf tournament. I had really looked forward to a little golf, a little beer. I was going to put some flowers on some graves and see some friends. The fact was, I was not ready for that. I got out of that, I had another funeral to attend.

Billy's life had been a mess. The lives of his family members were now really a mess. His wife lived those days on the verge of hysteria. Billy's mom was a rock. Billy's mom is a person from another age. I used to see her at Pike's once in a while. She had been a widower since sometime in the 60's. She was independent, like Howard Hughes was independent. She did what she damned well pleased, she dressed like she damn well pleased and she could care less what you thought of her. She had a solid cadre of friends who possessed mutual reverence. She had the VFW and she had the church. She was about 5'2" tall. She would walk into the bar, order a boilermaker or something similar. She always dressed the same. She wore blue jeans, cowboy boots with the pants tucked in. She wore a denim shirt and always a black cowboy hat. She would have one drink, say hi to anyone she knew and walk out, looking stern and straight-ahead. Billy's mom had no use at all for Billy's wife. It had been that way from the wedding day.

Billy had two daughters. All of Billy's friends were worried about the kids. Billy had not drawn up a will. The whole thing was a tangled mess. It took more than a year to straighten the thing out. As is turned out, Billy's life did not amount to much in the way of lasting wealth. It is probably just as well. His bride did her best to spend what there was, as quickly as she could. But all that was later. For now, another funeral. Several of Billy's good friends went through hell, but managed in spite of the bride, to have a nice ceremony. Billy was cremated and laid to rest finally. I swear it will be the last time I ever willingly view a body. My opinion of funerals is stated elsewhere. This funeral did nothing to change my opinion. It was an occasion to go to Fairbanks and to see some people that I had not seen in years. That was the only good thing. That, and I think that Billy, in all his efforts, had found his savior. For that, I am hopeful. Billy had worked two jobs at least, since he was sixteen. Billy needed a rest.

Becky and I drove back home. I often wondered what would have become of me had I not had Becky in these last ten years. We were kind of a mirror for each other to look into and see the truth. The truth always came with support. During the bad times, the support may have wavered during a couple of real bad times, but it was never abandoned. The overused term, "soulmate," is stale and almost a cliché. The concept of commitment is a more accurate term. It is simple and precise. If you have it, you have everything. If you lack it, your soulmate might someday fly off and mate with some other soul. Once you have committed to another person and that other person has committed to you, then you are finally able to become yourself. When you have accomplished that, you have a fighting chance to find happiness.

Becky has the ability to summon her sense of humor under most circumstances. I think a sense of humor is the most desirable of all human characteristics. It is essential to mental health in these complex times. So, driving home from Billy's funeral, we laughed at his memory. I told her about the time that Billy, two days out of the hospital, had thrown away his crutches. He then danced the night away with a girl he called "thunder thighs," so long ago in Johannesburg. I told her about the time that we were in Dubai. Billy was the project manager on this particular contract. He had rented a car. When it was time to turn it in, he had gone to the car rental company. "The rag-heads charged me a 50% surcharge. I told them I would be back in a minute, had one last thing to do," he said. Billy then went to the fish market, bought twenty pounds of fresh fish and locked the fish in the trunk. He left the car in the airport parking lot taking the key. It was about one hundred twenty degrees in the shade. "Tore up the credit card slip, paid them in cash." When Billy was in his twenties he was one of the most powerful men I had ever met. He matched it with a lust for life that somehow had gotten trampled on for twenty years. Trampled under the heels of the soulmate that God had provided him. He had been trampled but never beaten. I will miss Billy a lot. Becky cried but I didn't. I just thought of that last full kiss on the mouth that I had shared with Billy and knew he had had the last laugh.

One of the things I love to do is go dip netting on the Copper River. Alaskan residents can obtain a permit from the Fish and Game. This permit allows you to harvest twenty or so salmon, for personal use, from the Copper River, simply by using a net and dipping them out of the river. The Copper River flows into Prince William Sound near Cordova. It is the most spectacular river I have ever seen. It is a lot like what the Colorado River must have been like before all the dams. Becky and I try to go at least once a year. The trip turned into a complete failure. I fell in the river, only got about four fish and got a rude slap in the face. Becky was very upset. I was pissed off and disappointed. I couldn't even catch any goddamned fish. We argued. She cried and the whole episode was a disaster. Becky seems to be somewhat clairvoyant when it comes to my personal safety. She was very upset with me. At the time, I simply put the incident out of my mind. I simply wrote it off as another episode that played into the hands of the Black Witch. In fact, that day on the Copper River was to play a pivotal role. From that day forward I begin to change my strategy. I began to look inward. It was becoming apparent that the Witch was not the problem. The problem was me. I had loose ends I had to deal with.

I decided to no longer battle the Witch, but rather to discover the source of her power over me. Once I knew the source, I could deal with that. Then I could carve her up, starting with those piercing red eyes, the ones she implanted into the mirror in the morning, regularly nowadays. Then I could continue to cut her up, finishing with that evil, black heart that drummed and pulsed in my head. My bother-in-law says it's something called tinnitus. Maybe so, but on those days when it drowns out all else, I know it as the tambourine of the Black Witch. She slams and bangs that thing against my head for hours or even days, gangling out her siren song of hell. I didn't know any of these things that day as we drove the beautiful Glen Highway back to Anchorage. I will never know exactly how the mind works. I only know that, given a chance, your head is usually on your side.

Chapter V

LOOKING FOR SOME LIGHT

"I've been down so goddamn long that it
looks like up to me." The Doors

In 1984, my personal financial situation was at its peak. It had been in decline ever since. Wealth, or the lack thereof, is one of the primary ignition sources that drive that engine called stress. My stress engine had been incrementally increasing in RPM all of those fourteen years. The high-octane supply of fuel for that engine was the continuing failure of one business venture after another. The Black Witch would have you believe that there are many reasons for business failures, none of which is you. Partners, economy, bad luck, many reasons, but never you. Take away a delusion, the Black Witch is forced to retrench. The fact is that I had to admit that every reverse in my life was specifically my fault. The secret of an admission like this is, of course, to retain your confidence in the face of it. That is a big deal. The whole process takes time. Stress engines out of your control are another matter. Say the death of friends or family, or say the demise of a worldwide company that is the source of most of your personal cash flow. The timing of these events is, of course, another source of high-octane fuel.

In the summer of 1998 Southern Air began a decline that would force the termination of its operations. This company employed both Becky and me. Between our combined salaries, we were paying our bills and paying off all my latent debt. When it became evident we were both going to be out of a job, the Black Witch began to howl with glee. The shutdown of the company found Becky in Europe, me in Anchorage. One day we had a combined income approaching six figures, the next, we had zero. My personal company lost its main client, Southern Air, and plunged into a fountain of red ink. The first thing to go of course was the salaries of the owner, me. Becky is, by nature, a lot more practical than I am. But contrary to her nature, she accepted our situation stoically. I may be a realist, but I am also an optimist, when not operating under the influence of the Black Witch. You see, the worst thing that could possible happen, already had. Two dead kids, one dead parent and a dead friend. All in the span of a few years. Bankruptcy was a gentle breeze that blew in the wake of a tornado. What could they do next, kill us? Go for it. We stuck together, Becky and me. We disarmed that Witch of one of her more potent weapons, the stress linked to financial strain. We simply decided that we would get different jobs. If we were able to continue to service our monthly bills, fine. If not, so what? They couldn't kill us. Two people committed to each other, working together, are a far more formidable foe than one man is alone. I fell back on the one constant in my life for the past 25 years, the Lockheed Hercules. The new kid on the block, Lynden Air Cargo had a place for me. I would spend a lot of time out of town, but the cash would continue to flow. Becky now had a new skill. She was a trained, flight attendant. She soon found employment with one of the oldest and most respected airlines in Alaskan history, Reeve Aleutian Airlines. We took a cut, pay-wise, but we didn't miss any payments and we were able to avoid bankruptcy. Our little ground handling company retrenched also, we continued to lose money, but slowed the flow of red ink to a trickle.

Removing one of the Witch's weapons did not disarm her. Stoicism can either be a lethargic apathy, or it can be a mental refuge that keeps the Witch at bay while the forces of introspection plan an escape. Often, I think the first condition evolves into the second. That was the situation in my case. For a couple of months, I was content to just not give a shit, wait, and see what would happen next. When nothing bad did happen, I begin to plan my escape. Once I escaped from the clutches of the evil Witch, I could track her down and stake her to the ground and have my way with her. But first, I had to escape.

How many people take the risk and examine the deep recesses of the mind? Certainly men who have been in mortal combat. Others? There are those among us who possess a deep intellect and the moral courage to take an objective flashlight and cast a luminance on the subconscious. Men like Tennessee Williams, Byron, Edgar Allan Poe, Albert Camus.

What they find there often destroys them. Most people don't have the curiosity, the courage or, most often, any reason to look back there. There is a reason for that. Man is savage at heart. Self-preservation is the most basic of human characteristics. If staying alive is never an issue, a person never really understands their most basic characteristic. Men who fight other men for the right to survive are forced to study the animal within, sometimes to the point of their own demise. They are forced to consider that animal and contend with the resulting knowledge for the rest of their lives. Most people are not faced with life or death, when life means killing someone else. They will never know that animal. Self-preservation in one animal, sexuality in another. Sexuality is, of course, the left hand of self-preservation. You not only want to live, you are forced by instinct beyond your control, to try to mate with another human. Instinct determines attraction. The source of that attraction determines your place in the social order of whatever society you inhabit. Tennessee Williams, Oscar Wilde and others would not face near the personal tragedies nowadays as they dealt with in their own lifetimes. Biology and society at odds has been the bane of gay folks for centuries. I don't pretend to understand their dilemma. But I do understand that looking too carefully at the animal within is not for everybody. You might not like what you find in there. So, for most people, why look too closely? Why indeed? Because the Black Witch demands it, that's why. Either you want answers or you must be slave to the status quo. When the status quo finds you at the mercy of your emotions, a choice must be made.

If you fail at the normal measures of worth as dictated by our society, your accumulation of wealth, your fitness as a father, your fitness as a husband, and your contributions to the society at large, then you must justify your existence or fall prey to the Black Witch. At one time or another, I failed at all of the above. And understand, there are those people among us who relish the failure of others. The psychology of these people is unimportant. It is enough to know they exist, to identify them for what they are and thus render them impotent. The real enemy is not these pathetic parasites, it's not society, and it is not the Black Witch. The real enemies are those demons that hide in the dark caves of your mind. For most people, those demons, though they really do exist, lay comatose, and are left to decompose when the life spirit flees the body. These same demons are the minions of the Black Witch. She has the power to summon them from their slumber. The source of these demons, I believe to be the remnants of our ancestry. Pre-historic man existed. Whether modern man is just an evolvement of these beasts, or if a divine being somewhere along the line instilled an intelligence and spirituality into these beasts, or if literally, God dropped Adam naked and scared into a real garden, is of course the elemental question that mystifies theologians and intellectuals of every faction. The fact remains. Somewhere in our genes is a maniacal Hun, a bloodthirsty Mongol, or a member of one of the twelve tribes of Israel, all of whom murdered each other with abandon, raped and pillaged. There are elements of unenlightened beasts within us. If you are lucky, you never have to confront those beasts. If you are unlucky, you face them head-on in a war zone. If you are like me, then you have only a glimpse of the beast.

For me, this becomes an unfathomable dilemma. Because I wrote this book, I can now jump ahead to things the reader won't discover for many pages. But the real dilemma, as it turned out for me was the realization that these demons are a double-edged sword. In times of great stress, these demons are your saviors. But the vestige, some certain fragments of the ancestral beast within us, can litter our minds with dormant terrors inflicted on, or malevolence perpetuated by, those long ago ancestors. And a real question for me is, does that thread of genetics travel all the way back to sub-human beasts.

Shirley McClain and others make a case for past lives. Whether this is true or not, I think that there is an element of truth in it. I think that those qualities that allowed the people of those times to kill man and beast alike, commit acts of barbarism and deviant sexual behavior, are passed on genetically. It takes generations, if in fact it ever happens, for these traits to dissipate. So, hidden deep within the subconscious of all humans is the remnant of that beast that killed others with clubs and raped the weak. That remnant remains there, asleep, and there is nothing you can do about it. Who of you are without guilt for something that you have done that was not driven by lust of one name or another? It's the human condition.

The fact is then, if you never suffer a crisis of any kind, the normal mechanisms of human mental health block those dark features of the human animal that you would just as soon not admit you possess. Once, however, you are forced to question your own self-worth, then you are also forced to examine those dark areas of your nature to see if they, in some way, caused the misfortune that you now suffer. The realm of the

Black Witch. From this point it is only natural to consider the possibility that your failure is due to some sort of spiritual deficiency, if you are prone to believe that those qualities exist. If you are not prone to believe they exist, and if you are of a logical nature, then you are forced to wonder why so many seemingly intelligent people do believe. In either case, at least in my instance, I had to examine the possibility that such a spiritual warden might exist. The realm of the Black Witch. Of course, all of the above may in fact have no bearing on the true nature of man, but you have to start somewhere.

Hand-in-hand with the question of does spirituality exist, is the question posed by Camus: "There is but one truly serious problem, and that is suicide. Judging whether life is or is not worth living amounts to answering the fundamental question of philosophy." So who wants to start a sunny day out by saying, "Is life worth living?" If you have the courage to answer that question honestly, you must then try to come to a conclusion of what caused you to ask it. When you can't find that answer, you just move on and simply confront the question of spirituality. Next question: if there is a God, am I just suffering for my sins? Makes for a good day in a hotel room four thousand miles away from the one you love. In truth, it is better to do it there, out of the glare of her questioning face. Why go through an exercise like this? Won't this only perpetuate the doom and gloom? Either you want answers or you don't. If you want answers, then you must go in search of them. This, in turn, leads you to question your ancestry. Your parents. This is often an act of futility. What do you know about your parents that they didn't want you to know? There are some things you have learned from third parties, but most you know by observation. If you are critically objective, you have taken the first step. But here is where I part company with a lot of modern psychologists.

The fact is, that your worst behavior is not in the control of anyone but yourself. If you had parents like mine, then you were instilled with the basic tenets of right and wrong. You were provided with a good education and you were treated with love, for the most part. Whatever beast is loose in your head may have a genetic connection with your parents, but they also provided you with the tools to tame it. I speak only for myself. At no time in my life did I ever cross a self-imposed line of values with the aid of any type of psychological coercion, real or imagined, from my parents. A couple of my siblings insist that my alcoholic father cast some kind of psychological scar on my subconscious. If he did, I absolve him. I give it no credence. It may be a tragedy that I have no real respect for my father, but I look at it as a tragedy for him, not for me. And he's dead. Whatever amount of formative support I may have lacked from my dad, my older brothers, Jim and Bill mitigated it -- both as role models and in the activities they provided. Whatever the lack of supervision may have caused to my character was certainly made up for by my sisters Ila and later, Kathy. I hold more respect for my mother than any person I have ever met. Whatever dark forces live in my head, they are my responsibility. I was amply prepared during my youth by my extended family.

So what terrible things had I done that had caused pain or suffering to others? I'm not here to tell you. But I made an inventory. It turned out that excepting trivial instances where I may have violated societal rules of good behavior, I could name only a half dozen things I had done that may have caused harm to other people for no other reason than my own gratification. So where do you go from here? That depends on how you define spirituality. And how do you start on that quest?

At about this time, I begin to spend long periods working on the road. My first taste of this return to the traveling life was an inspiring one. There is a place in British Columbia called Bronson Creek. It is just across the border from Wrangell, Alaska. To get there, on most days due to low clouds, you must fly from Wrangell down the Stikine river to the confluence of the Iskut river and then up that river 30 miles or so. The runway at Bronson Creek begins at the river's edge and ends at the base of a cliff that rises a couple hundred feet. The whole area is cut out of some of the most beautiful real estate in God's creation. If a person like me needs to contemplate the nature of spirituality, there may be no better place on earth than this slice of the planet.

Wrangell, Alaska is located in Southeastern Alaska along the narrow stretch of land that borders Canada from Yakutat to Metlakatla. Its white man history dates back to the 1700's when the Russians were in pursuit of the fur of the sea otter. It is a place of huge hemlock and a clear, green, protected sea; the famous Inland Passage to the Alaskan mainland. It was to be my home for about two weeks. It is a small town of a few hundred souls. It had grown up on fishing, timber and minerals. Wrangell lies on that great stretch of timber known as the Tongass forest. Teddy Roosevelt designated this forest as a national park in the early 1900s. For most of the past century, the town's financial health was tied to the lumber mill located close by. The political winds of the 1980's have shut down most of the timber business hereabouts, so Wrangell, always a bit of a sleepy town, is now nearly comatose.

Lynden Air cargo is here to help shut down the Bronson Creek gold mine. The mine has been in operation for over twenty years. During that time, the mine has extracted untold quantities of gold ore, shipped it down the Stikine river to be loaded on barges in Wrangell and bound for Japan to be refined. Wrangell is about to lose another brick in their crumbling financial wall. The mine is played out. Our job is to remove all the heavy equipment from the mine and fly it to Wrangell. From here, the equipment will be loaded on barges. What cannot be flown out will be burned. The mine site is to be restored to its original condition, or nearly so. I am particularly happy to be here at this time in my life. The work is hard. It's hard work for a fit man in his twenties. For me, a man pushing fifty, it will be exhausting. But this is the kind of flying I love to do.

We are here to load thirty and forty thousand-pound machines into the back of the airplane. We then roar down the runway in all-out assault. The runway is hard-packed gravel of some five thousand feet. The runway ends abruptly at the edge of the fast-moving Iskut River. Once airborne, you must make a right turn-out upriver, gain some altitude and circle back downriver and fly the river back to Wrangell. One day out of ten or so, the sky may be clear, in which case you are able to fly a direct route over the mountains under a spectacular blue sky. The other nine days, the clouds form a solid barrier four or five hundred feet over your head and you fly at whatever altitude the elements allow. But it doesn't matter. The scenery at three hundred feet is just as spectacular and more revealing. Goats or sheep can be seen clinging to rocks on the jagged peaks. Black and brown bear roam at will in this still untamed land. Bald eagles in vast numbers comb the beaches for carrion. Then, there is the river valley.

The Stikine River is a fast-moving river of silty brown. It clears some as you move into Canada. But the forest is tall, green hemlock. This is a land of big trees. Big trees and big mountains. They have three varieties of salmon and they have steelhead and rainbow trout. Halibut are available in the green sea. If God exists, then you can certainly find him here. Why the big deal about God, spirituality, all of that?

The death of a child is an experience like no other. I felt a terrible guilt that I may, in time, be able to explain or deal with. The first step for me to try to make some sense out of it was to take something positive away from the carnage. I made myself a vow. I would take the late John Bernard Books' philosophy as my own. And more, I would disavow bullshit and look for the truth in things. So if a God exists, and if there is some kind of Grand Plan, then making sense out of a thing as senseless as the death of a child was a place to start. And since my sanity was tied directly to making some sense of Tasha's death, it wasn't really a choice in my case. So, starting here, I decided I had better answer truthfully when someone asked me if I believe in God. Do I? Well, like the great French philosopher Voltaire once said, "define your terms." That may sound like an easy thing. Not for me.

I started with the simple premise that spirituality is either the embodiment of God or the by-product. When I was a kid living in Vancouver, Washington, we got three TV stations, all broadcast from Portland, Oregon. I can't remember which station it was, but when they would end their broadcast day at about two in the morning, they would sign off with a poem by an American flyer, flying for England in WWII. On an August day in 1941 he took off in a Spitfire and rode it to 33,000 feet. Later that same day he wrote that poem. The final stanza is:

"Oh! I have slipped the surly bonds of Earth,
And danced the skies on laughter-silvered wing;
Sunward I've climbed, and joined the tumbling mirth
Of sun-split clouds,-and done a hundred things
you have not dreamed of,- wheeled and soared and swung
High in the sunlit silence. Hov'ring there,
I've chased the shouting wind along, and flung
My eager craft through footless halls of air...

Up, up the long, delirious burning blue.
I've topped the windswept heights with easy grace,
Where never lark, or even eagle flew-
And while with silent, lifting mind I've trod
The high untrespassed sanctity of space,
Put out my hand and touched the face of God.

Pilot Officer John Magee, Jr., RCAF

This guy, flying with the RAF, found his spirituality in an airplane, soaring through the clouds. At the low points in my life, every one of them that I can remember, if I were able, I would retreat to a place of solitude, away from town, somewhere in the woods. So if I'm going to find God, I'm going to find him in the woods. The woods to me is, and will always be, big trees, big mountains.

This whole God thing is such an impenetrable mental labyrinth. Christianity, the Bible all depends on a deep and total faith. The problem is that you are assaulted, via your five senses, with the chaotic symphony played daily by the hundreds of people who happen to inhabit your personal sphere. People you work with, people you respect, people of intelligence and integrity, who on a daily basis trash and disregard the basic tenets of this Christian religion. Your friends and colleagues rain havoc down on the teachings of the good book every day. Add to this, the incredible slaughter that is brought to us via the media. Daily slaughter and mayhem on a grand scale. In the face of all this, you must then make the effort to ascribe three thousand year-old words to the turbulent events of everyday life. This effort can be terribly futile. Add to that the words themselves. How can you take a three thousand year-old document, said to be originally scripted on stone tablets, and expect it to reign over a digital world. You might simply misconstrue the essence of the stone tablets. Those words were written in a different age for a different people.

Everybody keeps waiting for Jesus to reappear. He'd better do it pretty soon. For a lot of people the words written on a stone tablet are in need of an update. Either that or many people are doomed to hellfire, not because they are evil, but simply because those words of so long ago fail to cast any light on the situation they see that surrounds them. And as the chaos builds and widens, apathy is the natural result. The daily ranting of the iridescent tube flicking in the corner of almost every building nowadays has almost the quality of a deity for some. You can have whatever pleasure that excites you magically broadcast into the privacy of your own room. The only god you have to pay is the cable company. So for people like me, there is one escape. God exists, it is said, in every blade of grass, every tree, every mountain. To escape the chaotic symphony and have a shot at something immaculate, I had to retreat to nature, to the woods.

When I first got to Wrangell, I arrived ahead of the Hercules on a commercial flight. I then chartered a small airplane to Bronson Creek. I stayed there for three days, working with the Canadian miners, getting the sequence of the loads set up and the equipment ready to be loaded on the airplane. Let me take a few minutes here to talk about Canadians. Let me qualify that to encompass rural Canadians. Rural Canadians are Alaskans who live in a different country, or vice versa.

Big cities to me are an embodiment of the Chaotic symphony. It seems to me that sometime in the middle of the twentieth century, civilization began a process of regression. A process that was born in big cities in the Western hemisphere. At some point in time, when the people of rural beginnings began moving to the cities, they lost that basic tenet, not only of Christianity, but also of basic human nature. Love thy neighbor. Love thy neighbor for he will watch out for you and you for him. After being thrust into the chaos of a huge city, this is the first thing that people abandoned in order to survive. And civilization started to reverse its intended course. We live with the residue to this day.

At Bronson Creek, I was lucky enough to be immersed in the society of Canadian miners, and these are wonderful people. Bronson Creek was actually a little city of maybe a hundred people, men and women. They accepted me at once and offered only kindness and good humor. I lived with them for three days and enjoyed it immensely. These people possessed the good humor and good manners born of solid family values and wide-open spaces.

At night I was able to walk the length of the runway to the water's edge and just sit. This is rainforest. This is big trees and big mountains. The only sound was the rushing of the river and the breeze blowing through the trees. I sat there for three nights, waiting for God, Ed McMahon or the tooth fairy, whoever showed first. All three stayed away. You have to define him before you can find him. I didn't find God at that mine, not in the big trees.

What I did find, for the first time in many years, was that I had an open mind. So I decided that I would take this open mind out among the people and see what I could learn. I was already reading the Bible on a daily basis. I told myself I would also get a rudimentary knowledge of basic philosophy. But for now, I would enjoy my time in this paradise of big trees and big mountains. So after my three days in Bronson Creek, I flew back to Wrangell with the idea that my life was just starting. I was new, the world was new, but now I had a leg up. I was an experienced fifty-year-old man. I could easily separate the chaff from the wheat, the bull shit from the bull and so on. It was a day of low clouds as I sat next to a pilot in a single engine Piper and we flew back to Wrangell amongst the mountains, the trees and a mountain goat or two.

The crew I would be flying with was completely unknown to me. Chris, Henry, Scott and the mechanic, who has since left the company and whose name I have forgotten, were all Alaskans. During the time I had spent with Southern Air, the crewmembers were from all over the country, so as Forrest Gump once said, "You never know what you're going to get." Guys that had grown up flying in Alaska, for the most part, had pretty much the same background, so you knew what you were getting. Still, pilots are pilots. The most important quality of a pilot is self-confidence. Self-confidence breeds arrogance in some, humility in others. That, you can deal with. But if arrogance then bleeds over to self-importance, then you may have a problem. Any pilot worth his measure in my book, is interested in any information about the area in which he is flying. The source of that information is irrelevant, as long as it is good information.

Chris was a captain I had never met. I knew absolutely nothing about him. Now my well-being would be placed in his hands. So that first day when I saw him, I asked if he had ever been to Bronson Creek before. He answered, "No, but I saw the video." So I told him that I had been there and there were some things I could tell him about it. This was an important moment in our relationship. I had only one reason to tell him what I knew. So he would know. How he accepted that information would tell me a lot about his personality. Some captains somehow feel that once they have reached that high plateau, that only other captains, and maybe God, can add to their knowledge. So I told him what I knew. He listened carefully and attentively. That told me all I needed to know about his personality, the only other question was his ability.

The first flight with any crew that is unknown to me is cause for a little tension. When that first flight is down a cloud-covered valley, a few hundred feet off the water to a destination none of them had ever seen before, it only serves to heighten that tension. So it was on this first day. We were working our way up the Stikine River. Shortly after we entered Canada, the Iskut River dumps into the Stikine from the southeast. Here is the first important decision. The Iskut River is much narrower.

Once committed to this river, there are only a couple of places to turn around because the valley is too narrow. We flew by the confluence and took a good look up the river. The clouds were solid at about six hundred feet. There was no evidence of dense fog; just mist, like looking into a room where one person is smoking. It's times like these when you feel pretty helpless and just turn over your fate to other people. The three flight crewmembers talked it over., The mechanic and I just stared at each other. Chris finally decided to take a look. There was one place about two miles upriver to turn around. So, we committed. But the cloud ceiling held and we worked up the river at flaps 50%. This allows you to go much slower than with the flaps all the way retracted. We are motoring up upriver at about 150 knots.

This was going to be a good day though. We made it all the way to the runway without incident. Chris had been briefed by the Chief Pilot about what to expect at this point. He executed a sweeping turn around an island in the river and landed perfectly, the runway ending at the base of a three hundred foot mountain. There was wreckage of two airplanes that littered the side of the runway. This particular strip had claimed seven airplanes in its twenty years of existence. It was a test of the skill of any pilot, but the stress of any potential flying danger was now mitigated. I was flying with an excellent, competent team. The ensuing days now had the weight of some tension removed. These guys were OK. So our little project had begun.

I had been out of the flying business for some months when I found myself in Wrangell. My body had grown soft from inactivity. All that changed immediately. We worked hard that first day. I think we did four round trips. We were loading big equipment; thirty-thousand pound generators, huge steel equipment, and mining vehicles. The rollers we use on the airplane are about one one-hundred-eighty pounds apiece, the portable truck ramps about seventy pounds each. Everything is tied down in the airplane with big chains that weigh about thirty pounds apiece and I was out of shape. I was completely done in at the end of that first day. The next two days were more of the same.

So let me take you on a little Herc ride. We had just loaded forty-three thousand pounds of freight on board. The logistics guy from the mine was using the manufacturer's published weights for the most part. We only had to guess on things like pickup trucks and miscellaneous steel. This particular trip we had loaded a thirty thousand pound generator, a bucket from a front-end loader, a welder and a small tool shed. Forty-three thousand pounds, more or less. Well, a little side story.

Recently, I had been in a village on the west coast of Alaska. The Hercules community is a fairly small society. During the seventies, when the pipeline construction was in full swing, Alaska was teeming with oil camps and geological survey camps, in addition to mining and construction companies that have been a constant customer of the Hercules aircraft all these thirty years. The people who came into contact with the Herc in those pipeline days numbered in the thousands. These days, most of those people are gone. Dead or retired or moved on. A few old-tiners can still be found. Guys that for one reason or another, often times ex-wives, have postponed retirement or simply cannot afford it. The gala parade had all passed into history, but there are a few of us left behind, kind of cleaning up the parade grounds. When you run into one of these guys it's usually at some very remote site and he is there because he has worked with airplanes before.

So when you get off the airplane and there stands a guy you spent two weeks with twenty years ago in a place called Eagle Creek, you stop and shoot the breeze for a few moments. Then he says, "You remember the time that you hauled that 966..." out of such and such a place. "Remember the captain was all pissed off because he thought we had overloaded him. Well, I decided it doesn't matter anymore. Let me tell you why that loader was so heavy." A 966C is a wheeler loader made by Caterpillar. With bucket and forks and fuel it weighs about forty-three thousand pounds, always has, always will. Then he tells me the story. "It was cold as hell that winter, we were having trouble with the tires. Got tired of fixing flats, so we filled up all four tires with foam. We didn't think about it when it was time to fly it out. But after the captain raised so much hell, we got to thinking about it. We ran it over the scales when we got it to Prudhoe. Damned thing weighed almost fifty-thousand pounds. Who would of thought that foam was so heavy?"

So, like I say, we had on about forty-three thousand pounds. More or less. We are now sitting at the end of a five thousand foot runway with that weight tied down behind us. Staring at us from a mile away is a raging brown river. The end of our runway. Each crewmember has their own thoughts. My mind is visually going over each tie down, on each individual piece of cargo in the back, wondering what I had forgotten to do, and wondering for the last time what the cargo really weighs. Then the fun begins.

Let me tell you what I knew about the crew to this point. Chris, the captain, was in his late thirties. He had been flying old airplanes in Alaska for some time. He was stocky, about my height. He had a head full of hair and a walrus mustache that framed a mouth full of teeth. He was a happy-go-lucky guy with a ready joke and was always smiling. Henry, the co-pilot, was tall, thin and laconic. He smoked lots of cigarettes, had a biting wit and a great sense of humor, in his 40s, maybe a little cynical. Scott, the Flight Engineer, was about the same age as Chris. He didn't say too much. He was always watching though. All three of them didn't quite know what to make of me. My professional reputation at that time was pretty good. I had been in this business for a long time. My reputation was one thing, but once the throttles are pushed forward to the max power setting, your reputation could be ruined forever along with five lives. Often, when the co-pilot is filing his flight plan over the radio, the guy taking his flight plan will ask "How many souls on board?" Not people, souls. That has always intrigued me. When you fly for a living, your reputation is reborn every time those throttles are advanced on a takeoff roll. Another thing that I figured out along the way is that there are two distinctly different things about flying. Flying is a job, or it can be complete freedom. It can't be both. If you fly for a living, you have to be part of a crew. If you fly as a pilot, in your own airplane, it is the most complete freedom that I have ever experienced.

The captain, Chris, calls for full power. This instant is an interesting and telling time. This instant defines professionalism. Outside of whatever preparation was done to this point, whatever is about to happen in the next few minutes is the only important thing in your life. Whatever happened before this moment doesn't matter now, and it won't matter again until it is important again. Maybe five minutes. During the first few moments of any flight, the only important thing in your life is the airplane. If you are part of the crew, you depend totally on the rest of the crew. At this point that includes the mechanic and me. Did we do our jobs? After a few seconds though, it's just the three of them. I am left to watch. It's not three steely-eyed aviators. It's three guys a lot like you, who if they are professional, will do the best they can to deposit your soul safely back on terra firma without any other consideration.

The flight engineer, Scott, sitting between, and slightly recessed from the two pilots, pushes the four throttles forward to the full power setting. The sound changes dramatically as the power is advanced. It changes from a whine as the prop is just slapping at the air, to a thrumming sound as it bites into it. The airplane begins to shudder at being restrained by applied brakes. "Max power," announces Scott. Chris releases the brakes and the airplane lurches forward. Anything bad that will happen in the cargo compartment, my domain, will normally happen now. I hear nothing. I am a spectator now. Basically, the lives of five people now rest in the two hands and feet and between the ears of the captain.

What makes a good captain? Certainly not smooth takeoffs and landings. A good captain is totally aware of all pertinent factors that have any influence on a particular flight. Weather, runway condition, etc. The most important factors, however, are the knowledge of the capabilities of the airplane and his own capabilities and limitations. Then he must make good decisions based on all this knowledge. But he must be, first and foremost, self-confident.

After the initial lurch, the plane starts down the runway gathering speed. This is a guess, but I have watched Chris walk the runway several times. I think he has marked a spot on the runway as the go/no go spot. After the plane has passed a certain spot on the runway, no aborted takeoff can be performed. We will be unable to stop before we get to the river. So, now we are hurtling down the runway, gathering speed. "Eighty knots." This from Henry. "V 1," again from Henry. The roar of the engines is somewhat muted now, the airplane is bouncing along and my eyes are fixed on the airspeed indicator. Once it approaches one hundred knots, I know we are OK. "Rotate." Henry again. We lift off a hundred feet from the water's edge and we are flying at about one-hundred-ten knots, just feet above the rushing brown water. I am pushed back and down into my seat, the "G" force settling upon you as the airplane transitions to flight. "Positive Rate." Henry. "Gear Up." Chris. The airplane shudders as the gear is coming up and the door closes. "V2." Henry. "Flaps up." Chris. Scott, this entire time, is keeping an eye on the power settings, engine oil pressures and temperatures. He is looking for anything that might be amiss. We fly upriver and circle an island, reach whatever height the clouds allow and turn back downriver. And we spend the next thirty minutes or so flying through a valley of spectacular scenery. Mountains reach up several hundred feet above us, just feet from the end of the wingtips. This kind of flying is as good as it gets for me. We land in Wrangell, unload and head for the barn. A good crew is a thing of beauty. A bad crew the opposite, your worst nightmare. A compromised crew is a death wish. I am now part of a good crew.

Chapter VI

"She is to know, not to understand" Dick Scott

The wanton nature of the Black Witch is like a nightmare. The memory of it fades after a few days and leaves you totally unprepared for the next sortie. Those first few days in Wrangell, the beauty of the country, the physical nature of the job, cast that Black Witch from my thoughts. So when I awoke in the hotel room, after the third day of intensive flying, I slowly gained consciousness to the feeling of anxiety. My upper body ached. The room was dark. Outside my window, black clouds scudded only a hundred feet off the water. Fog enshrouded the entire harbor area, hiding the fishing boats in its solid gray mass. A gray mass gripped my heart as well. The gray, veined hand of the Black Witch.

Just the effort of sitting up was like dabbing your tongue against an abscessed tooth. The dull ache of overused muscles intensified in this first small effort. I was used to these mornings, my aching upper body would normally retreat under the sedative of the coming day's physical exertion. Not today. Today that aching would follow me like a hungry dog. The airport was only a mile or so from my hotel room. We were socked in today. A phone call to Chris confirmed this. We were on a weather hold.

Today would be a bad day. A day of introspection amid the throbbing of a dull mortality. It would be the portent of many such days to come. The battlefield of the Black Witch is a dynamic psychic venue. The psychic nature of the battle renders it as an away game; you always battle on her home turf. Tedium is the unfamiliar surface. Anxiety it the abusive, taunting crowd. Depression is an endless road trip facing an opponent who has routed you ten straight times.

So it is with a resigned rote-ness that I get up and start the routine. Breakfast with the crew. A long walk along the windy dock. Back to the room to read seven pages of King James. Stare at four walls. Back outside to do a languid walk through nearly deserted streets. Wrangell is a logging town, was a logging town. The sawmill is shut down, the chainsaws silent. It is October. The cruise ships are gone. The stores remain open, more from habit than any hope for a profit. The town has a fifties feeling about it. Like maybe the economic high water mark was reached in the last part of that decade. The tide of intervening years, a receding tide of discretionary income, has left the town to resemble a fossil from another era. The kids, when they appear, are like pool balls. They bounce around town like they have been hammered by a cue ball. They hit hard against the cushion of the small town confines and careen off in another direction. First at the hamburger stand, then in a knot of cars next to the hotel, then off into the cloaking fog. Full of life, but just trapped on the pool table of a small town. I wonder how many of these kids will still be here in five years, how many will make their lives here? The townspeople, I love. Small-town people. After the first day, everybody knows who you are and what you are doing in town. They accept you at once. Not trust you maybe, but accept you with kind words and broad smiles. These are hardworking people trapped in hard times, but resilient and optimistic.

The weather is like an oppressive heavy cloud. It is exactly that. The mist is the ghost of water. As you move through it, you are the seed around which that mist condenses. You gather moisture in long, cumulative strides. Soon it is running in rivulets down your repellent Carhartt jacket and soaking into your blue jeans. Your work boots are a sodden firmament against the glassy pavement. Your spirits lie somewhere between the two.

Back in the room, the TV sits in one corner like a seductress who resides in a rundown trailer court. You pick up the remote, fondle it really, with something like the piquing of your dormant adolescent hormones and are rewarded with the sight of two obese female titans dueling for the affections of a backwoods Romeo. Jerry Springer is blasting late 20th century anthropology into the cosmos. You run through the available detritus that is basic cable TV, three times. Then in resignation, you sit down in silence to play solitaire with the Black Witch.

The book you tried to read yesterday has been mysteriously altered. It had, just yesterday, contained words that magically morphed into living images and then broadcast those images onto a screen in your head. The broadcast was a true story of two cowboys from Wyoming who traveled to British Columbia in the early part of the past century. The broadcast was narrated in the words of a simple man who had witnessed the taming of that frontier. Words, simple but elegant … yesterday. Today, those same words, when fed into the mental projector, jammed the device, only white flickering light made it to the screen today. After ten minutes, solitaire with the Witch was no longer an option. I called Chris and he said there would be no flying today. Daylight was running out, the weather was continuing to worsen. "Go have a beer," he said.

I left the room minutes later and walked through the forming rain for about three blocks. I turned and walked into a dark room with a wooden floor, a large horseshoe bar and a jukebox. I decided to drive a stake into the heart of this day, right here and right now. The room was empty. I sat for a few minutes alone before she appeared.

Some people say that a defining moment in a man's life is when he makes love for the first time. I think there are many such defining moments. I think one of the most important of such moments is when a man learns to value women for who they are. That point in a man's life where he sees a good-looking woman for the first time and sees, not a potential sex partner to be evaluated, rejected out of hand, or accepted as a potential body to pursue, or at least lust over, but sees instead another human being, a universe of untold experience. When he looks into the eyes of a woman and sees knowledge there, a wealth of viewpoints and perspective. That, I think, is not only an important defining experience, but also the last obstacle to adulthood and a pathway to wisdom. Some men, or boys really, seem to achieve this at an early age. Others never do. For me, this ability came relatively late. My wife Becky has provided an inviolable relationship for me. To violate that sanctum is a proposition so preposterous to me that it precludes consideration. Conversely, it has allowed me to get to know other woman a lot better than I would have in the past.

Her name has been lost to me. She lit up the dark room as she served my beer. I put Marty Robbins on the jukebox, and as he sang about the West Texas town of El Paso, I started a conversation with her that was to last intermittently for a couple of hours. A physical description of her is unnecessary. Her face was equal parts character and beauty. She wore blue jeans and white blouse. Her smile knocked down all barricades. We had Fairbanks in common, so we started with that. I nursed my beer and fed the jukebox. Dr. Hook, Patsy Cline, Waylon Jennings. On the wall over the jukebox, I was startled to see a picture of a Hollywood power couple. It looked like it had been taken in this very bar. I asked the barmaid about it and she said, yeah, the couple kept a boat here and showed up occasionally in the summer. They were nice people who liked the fact that they were left alone in this town.

The afternoon melted away amidst the strains of the steel guitar and simple melodies of real old rock and roll. The barmaid told me a little about the town and a little about her own life. Her husband was a fisherman. They had good years and bad years. But she had learned to love this town, and the town's woes were her woes. She seemed resigned to the timber industry's demise. Wrangell sits in the middle of the federally owned Tongass National Forest. This particular national treasure is currently a political football. The Alaskan legislative delegation is being slowly pushed back towards their own goal line on this issue. The conservation lobby is winning that battle. The people of Wrangell, the real football being kicked around, are pretty stoic over their fate; the losing game being played out in their back yard. The chainsaws will remain silent.

The afternoon drifted into evening. I saw no reason to return to my empty hotel room. Henry, the co-pilot, walked in and sat down next to me. It was full dark now. Henry said the weather didn't look like it was going to break any time soon. We were looking at an indefinite number of weather days. We were on a pretty tight schedule to finish this project. If we didn't move all the loads in another week, we were committed elsewhere and would have to come back to Wrangell at some later time.

Like me, Henry had suffered the failure of a business. He, on a much grander scale than I. He told his story and I told mine. The 1980's in Alaska was a time of lots of money floating around along with all the things that money could buy. The evening wore on. The other two crewmembers came in. I think that one of the things I had enjoyed most in my flying career was the diverse nature of the crewmembers I had met over the years. Most had some things in common. They were smart and they were talented. Most had at least a touch of wonder lust. The joy of the excitement of life.

I once saw Neil Young in concert. I was a long way from the stage. But if you cut all Neil's hair off, that's what Henry looked like. He smoked lots of cigarettes, had a sarcastic wit that you wondered about until he smiled and blew his own cover. Scott talked less and watched more. He has a sense of humor that had a bite to it. He wasn't afraid to use it on the other two. Chris was a no bullshit guy who papered the air with his view of flying, management, the girl behind the bar and Patsy Cline. It all sounded good to me. Of course there were a few flying stories. We had a couple more drinks and then headed, en-mass, back to the hotel. The weather was now an envelope, the darkness merely giving borders to the rain cloud we walked through. Now is that time of day that you most dread when you are living on the road.

Life on the road. When your job takes you from one out-of-the-way place to another with no pattern, events dictated by whatever crises or project comes up, it is a wonderful thing. A wonderful thing if you are a young, single man. Every day is a new adventure; new people, places, most of these places you have never heard of. Lubumbashi, Hassi Massaud, Francistown, Lobatsi, Kano, Ray Point, Ikpikpuk, Midway in Oman, Wrangell in Alaska. If you have been doing this same job for twenty-five years, and for the most part are now just retracing old steps, it is a different matter. Being married changes things immensely. Now that long walk down a darkened hallway to room 214 is just purgatory. Tonight is going to be OK though. When you are alone at last, alone again, attitude is everything. Taking a good attitude to bed when you are on the road might be the single most important thing you do all day.

I had met a kind woman who had turned a dour day around with her humor and her grace. Marty, Dr. Hook, Waylon, Willie and the others, had breathed some substance into the day's emptiness. Even Patsy, who went walking after midnight in the moonlight, had sucked some of my forlornness into her song. I really liked the guys I was flying with, and so as the day wore on, things had gotten better. I had drunk enough to be reflective, not introspective, a vital difference. So now when I walked into the confines of four walls, it was with a mellow resignation. The pervading gloom of the dying day was like the mental smell of a dead rat that you cannot find. It's in the room somewhere but you can't find it. But that mental smell, that dead rat gloom, was only ankle-deep on this night. I waded through the gloom to the large window facing the harbor with the eyes of a jaded romantic, not those of a skeptic.

The window was a thousand prisms of beaded and sweating raindrops. Beyond, the wharf was lit with the ghostly pall of four or five yellow lights. The pregnant cloud acted as a kind of diffuser/reflector of those smoky yellow lamps. Gray, wispy fog was drifting by like the lost souls of drowned fishermen. How many times had I looked out of a hotel room in places foreign to me and beheld the soothing grace of the saving sea. The sea is vital in my life. I don't plan on ever living very far from it. Some of my earliest memories are of walking along the ocean at Long Beach, Washington. There was an old shipwreck that was mostly buried in the sand. A wooden victim of some long ago storm. Beyond that wreck, a limitless beach stretched in both directions to the limits of a six year old's imagination. White waves crashed into boiling foam that rushed up and covered your ankles in frigid bubbles, hissing at you before slithering away. Those waves would play with you for hours: they never tired.

Despite all his flaws, my dad could tell a good story. In those most cherished of childhood memories, I remember being at the beach and him telling stories of storms that conceived waves as big as that telephone pole over there, higher than that building, he would say. How those waves would steal the big glass balls they sold in the curio shop, steal those balls from Japanese fisherman and wash them up on the beach here, five thousand miles away. Glass balls as big as basketballs. He had been in the merchant marine during the big war and had seen some of those waves. He told a good story. Mom said most of those stories were bullshit, the only cussword I ever heard from her until many years later. But they were still good stories, true or not. I would stare across that water forever it seemed, hoping to see Japan someday. And some day I got to see Japan. Dad told a good story and he loved the ocean. He gave those things to me, among all his failures. I wondered if I had done as well for my dead daughter.

It turns so easily. The mental rat smell was up to my knees now, though still at bay. I called Becky and we talked for some time. We hate being apart nowadays. The wreckage of my life had forced me onto the road again. I had found the woman I needed. I now needed the means to live with her full-time. After I hung up I sat and stared out the window. I climbed into bed, a good six inches above the smelly gloom and lay down, hoping for the best.

I woke up in a dark room. I came to consciousness slowly. I smelled for the rat. He was not there. I lay for some time staring at the ceiling. The rat had been flattened, crushed. Maybe it was by the same weight that now bore down on my chest. The pressure there released, slowly, like when they remove the leaden vest after completing an X-ray, only done in extra slow, slow motion. Dread swelled up in my head now. It filled the empty space of the just departed dream.

I was in this same bed in this same room. The air had been made of mercury. It pressed me down to the bed, pinned me there. I couldn't move a foot, not a hand or even a finger. My head weighed three hundred pounds. She had stood motionless by the side of my bed, my dead daughter. No expression, save a blankness in her eyes. With a Herculean effort I had opened my mouth to speak. The words made it to my mouth but were crushed there. Tasha stood there waiting for me to speak. I tried again. Nothing. She simply stared at me. I studied her eyes trying to understand. She could have been looking at me or she could have been blind. No recognition, no emotion. She wasn't sad. I didn't know what she wanted. She left me then, somehow. Just left. She didn't disappear; she just wasn't there any more.

I lay there breathing evenly. I wanted for all the world to have a drink then. I did not. I got up and walked to the window and drew back the curtains. It could have been six am, or it could have been noon. The inside of the window was left with watery lines when I ran my hand down its surface. My fingers came away wet. Wrangell was still living in the envelope of a large gray cloud. I couldn't even see the lights on the wharf. I got dressed and walked out onto that invisible wharf. An hour or so later, I went back into that room. What good is a Bible, or any book, in the face of a day like this? Still, I read those seven pages, or rather, the words passed by my eyes. I didn't remember a single word of it. There would be no God, no tooth fairy and surely no Ed McMahan on this day.

Then the phone rang. It was Bob. Bob is the guy who owns the ground handling company that is doing the ground support for our airplane. He owns the rental van we are driving. He thinks he has called

Chris, the captain, but got me instead. He tells me its zero/zero at the airport. Zero forward visibility, zero distance between the bottom of the clouds and the runway. He asks me to let Chris know. I tell him I will. Then he says, "You play cribbage?" I told him I did. "Well, if you don't have anything better to do," he chuckles at that, "come on out." I tell him I'll get some breakfast and see him in a couple of hours. I met the crew for breakfast downstairs. It is definitely another weather day. Chris says he will run me out to the airport after breakfast, which he does.

Bob is one of those wild-eyed Alaskan developers you have heard so much about. He's pushing sixty real hard, maybe already pushed clear through that barrier. He was raised in Pennsylvania and came here to Wrangell forty years ago. He's got a picture of Ronald Reagan on the wall. Bob was a schoolteacher, later a principal. He has been engaged in the education of Wrangell's children for most of thirty years. Now he rents a few cars, loads a few airplanes, does this and that. With the closing of the mine whose equipment we are now flying out, he will lose one of his streams of revenue. He has been unloading ore from airplanes for twenty years now. A nice little sideline. But that is gone soon. A few bucks gone too. Bob has invested his entire adult life in this community. As the economy erodes around him, he lets seep out, a little fire.

There is a joke around Wrangell that there should be a bounty for REI clothing tags. This joke is in reference to the penchant for the outside environmental people who show up in town dressed in the latest outdoor chic. "Outside" in the preceding sentence meaning anyone who resides in the "lower 48" states, otherwise known as the Continental US. Outdoor chic, meaning REI, Northface, etc. Bob is a grumpy old guy in a baseball cap, Woolrich shirt and blue jeans. He has taught most of the people in this town under the age of forty, and many more who have left. He is angry that they are shutting down the woods and the mill. He is angry that his town is at the mercy of interests that live farther away than some foreigners. He is angry at the arrogance and condescending nature of those interests. He is angry that this town has lost the ability to control its own destiny. Bob is an angry man, a wild-eyed angry man who is so irresponsible in his politics that two generations of Alaskans have entrusted the education of their children to him. He tells of the old days when John Wayne would show up every summer. A good guy, a beautiful boat, and so on.

But this morning, the talk has a serious edge. A couple of "kids," guys in their late teens, are late in returning from a trip to the hot springs up the Stikine (pronounced Stickeen) River. There is no real panic -- not yet -- just the hard edge of concern in the voices. There are some worried parents. Soon the whole town will know. In the meantime, we play cribbage as a parade of townspeople drop in to say hi or play a hand. Bob's language is laced with invective and mild profanity. The morning wears on. Sometime about noon, the kids show up. Only then does the talk turn to similar incidents that didn't turn out so well.

Cribbage was my mom's favorite card game. Whenever I was home, when she was still living, it was a daily ritual. My game is pretty good. The games between Bob and me are pretty close when the cards run even. When not, Bob skunks me. But then I have my shots too. Bob goes to Reno every year for a national cribbage tournament. That tournament is coming up and I get the feeling that Bob has been playing a lot lately. There is a period of time when Bob has to stop and run an errand or two. At these times I just sit in his office and look out the window and drink his coffee. The day passes in this manner and my mood improves with the ticking of the clock. Late in the afternoon, the mechanic shows up. He has to do a daily maintenance inspection of the airplane. Bob takes off for home and says to lock up when we go. I help the mechanic for a while. He tells me to go on in, he has to finish the paperwork. I'm wet as hell by now, so I agree.

I walked into Bob's office, sat down and stared out towards the ocean. What happened next will remain a mystery to me for all time. I have since wondered about the state of people's minds when extraordinary events occur to them. I know that biblical visions were often preceded by times of fasting. Certain American Indians enhance their ceremonies with the use of hallucinogens. Both of these examples seem to me to suggest that altering the mind in one way or another was a precedent to plumbing its depths. I have wondered if my mental state contributed to what happened, or was wholly responsible for a delusion of some kind. I sat down in Bob's office and was just staring out of the window into the total blackness of the inside of a cloud at night. Instantaneously, there is an intense beam of light that pierced the blackness like a spotlight. A laser-like intensity stabbed through the blackness, straight into the room where I was sitting. This laser of light illuminated one book on the upper shelf of Bob's office. Swear to God.

After half a second, the light is extinguished. Poof, gone. Dutifully, I went to the bookshelf and picked up the highlighted volume. I make a note of the title and put it back. The author of that book and I share a common name. The mechanic comes in then and we lock the door and head back to town. We join the crew for a couple of beers, then walk through the drizzle back to the hotel. I said nothing to them about the little incident.

The sun will shine tomorrow and we will do five trips to the mine. A week later we will leave Wrangell with about twenty some loads left unmoved. We are headed for Detroit to move some car parts. The months between Wrangell and the New Year will find me mostly on the airplane and away from my wife. My life wears on in this manner. Good days, bad days, but they are mostly days spent away from my wife and those kinds of days blow my soul around like a wind vane. I'm a fifty-year-old guy who got caught in the spotlight of a once romantic job, a job that once was the promise of my youth. That spotlight now just frames me like a deer frozen in the glare of headlights, somehow unable to run away.

The book. I found a copy in a bookstore in Detroit. I read it thoroughly, twice. Then I threw it away. It was a quasi-religious, mostly psychiatric prescription for dealing with life and loss. It seemed to me that it was written by a guy trying to push troubled folks into sessions with a psychiatrist, the author's profession. It was some kind of cosmic joke. God had the wrong guy, or I had the wrong God. I could not buy what that author was trying to explain. What he had to say, his conclusions just did not speak to me. There had to be something more than what that guy was selling.

But I had left Wrangell with the idea that I would, with an open mind, try to digest the Bible. I would also look into other philosophies, maybe other religions. One stroll through a large bookstore revealed a simple truth. A soul, searching for meaning, could spend the rest of his life in such a pursuit, at a purely intellectual level. There is so much material that it is simply overwhelming. I took the perspective that a soul in search of truth would somehow be guided, or the whole concept was corrupt. So with that in mind, I spent the next year or so scratching the surface of the Christian religion, some of the more renowned philosophers, a little of the new age line of thought that had intrigued me years before, but mostly I just drifted back to the incident.

Not the spotlight incident, but the other. Through all of this though, I looked around and tried to keep an open mind.

That next year on the road was spent mostly in Detroit. It turned out that this particular contract offered a lot of free time. We were on call mostly and would go days without working. It left a lot of time for reading. And a lot of time for depression. Days on end, spent with the Black Witch. At this time I think my pursuit of some sort of spiritual poultice was as much about filling my hours with something productive. Something positive. So in a way, the process of studying the Bible and these other books was, in fact, some sort of mental therapy that probably was just as important as the pursuit of answers.

Depression, I am sure, must have been considered an animate demon in the middle ages, before the age of enlightenment. A demon. Your body and mind in the possession of an evil spirit. Today, depression is diagnosed as a chemical imbalance brought on by stress, emotional distress and a myriad of other factors. Bullshit! Depression is when your mental faculties are in the possession of an evil spirit. Whatever the inner workings of the mind consist of, the images that rattle around inside your head are what you must deal with. Drugs can intoxicate you, drugs can sedate you, drugs can provide you with hallucinations. But what happens inside your head is real. So if a drug alters what happens in there, then your reality is altered. What goes on inside your head is your reality. If there are drugs that change your personality so you don't kill somebody, those drugs are just medical policemen. The reality inside your head that has been altered so you don't kill somebody is still your reality. For some, the word "demon" is preferable to the word "imbalance." When a demon lives in your head it is a demon god dammit, not an imbalance. If you choose to kill that demon with drugs for the sake of civility or appearance, that is a choice that is made.

So, you wake up on Christmas Eve morning, alone in some hotel room in a city that has lost part of its soul. You look out the window at a pale sky, dirty snow in an upscale ghetto on the south side of Detroit. You take your morning walk along a sidewalk and carefully step over the syringes lying there. You go back to your room and stare at three whiny rich bitches arguing about winter fashions on some plastic TV soap opera and you feel like shit. At least you didn't have to buy your daughter a Christmas present because she's dead. None of it's your fault. It's all because of some chemical imbalance. Take some pill dude.

Interlude with Sherry, part six

"And so this is Christmas, I hope you have fun, The near and the dear ones, The old and the young." John Lennon

Everybody has gone away. I'm sitting alone in a room, the perfect Christmas scene is pasted to the outside of the window. My sister has just left, she spent the entire afternoon putting up the tree. It's a beautiful tree. I sent Bill out to get some booze. Ben is at a party with the boys. I'm holding a collage of Tasha's pictures in my hand. And God damn it, the other song comes into my head. I am so God damned lonesome that I am crying. Buckets. What on earth could make a God so damn cruel that I have to go through this? I got some pills, but I can't take them. I got to get through this, I must get through this. The little shit Justin comes running up and jumps into my lap. Hurt is an abscess tooth throbbing in my heart. I brush the red hair from his face. "Why you crying again mommy?"

Christmas is over. Your head is full again. Full of things that infect you. Things that infect you and prey upon you. You wake up to another god damned chemical imbalance. There aint no chemical imbalance loose in my head, what's loose in my head is a god damned virus and a god damned demon. The damned virus is making me crazy and the god damned demon wants to do something about it. So chill dude, make some sense out of it. OK, you believe in demons. A little bizarre, but hey, the paranoia is shrinking. Let's run with this. OK, demons are real, then, OK, if demons are real then spirits are real. Spirits ward off the demons. OK, let's take it from here. So let's search for God based on the simple premise that if I could define and nail down that immaculate spirit that would ward off the evil demons in my life, then the Black Witch could be shown to the door.

The saving of my soul was at this juncture in my life, simply gravy. Let me say here also that I have never been a particularly spiritual person, never saw a need. You all have heard tales of depression, such a debilitating condition that some people are made to live in darkened rooms, or even to kill. This Black Witch thing was not like that at all. Through a series of very traumatic events, I had become a person who no longer enjoyed life. I was simply just living it. Not trying real hard. Something inside of me was saying that if you are just sucking up oxygen, then you are out of character, certainly. Maybe no longer valid. I had also lost control of my emotions, able to break down at the first strains of certain songs. I was not in control of my life. I was just being swept along on the tide of events. I just figured that if so many people gave such credence to this idea of spirituality, that maybe I had entirely missed the boat. Maybe there was an answer to this pervasive emptiness that could take me back out of the woods into the sunshine. Of course my character demanded that whatever solution I found had to be logical, had to make sense. Then the day after Christmas you wake up a half crazy man. Then you think, I need this job, I got to take care of my wife. I need to take some sort of conventional road or it's all over. So over the course of the next several months, I went looking for answers.

A good writer has the ability to allow you to put life into ideas that have been wallowing around in your head. When you read something on a printed page, and it mentally captures and gives form to a thought that has never really crystallized before, it's like finding a friend of the spirit. You are no longer alone. One of the first ideas I discovered among some renowned philosophers was one by Henry Spencer. And it speaks to people with concrete and absolute beliefs in Christianity, or any religion for that matter. Paraphrasing him somewhat, it goes like this: Like everybody else, I am one of the myriad of agents of that unknown Deity. My beliefs are a product of God, and by his immaculate will, I am able to say these words. The reasons for this are of course His providence only. So, if in my heart I deviate from classical Christian beliefs, God made me do it.: If that provokes some people to write me off as the Devil, then I know for a fact that I am more right than they are. Because we can also go to Corinthians 15:10, "But by the Grace of God I am what I am: and his Grace which was bestowed upon me was not in vain...." I took Mr. Spencer's prescient insight as a guide.

The recent deaths of my mother, my daughter and my friend, Billy, has been cause enough for me to finally read the Bible. My brother, Ralph, is one of my nine brothers and sisters who were on the death watch when my mother lay dying. Ralph was the only one of the nine on a mission. He spent the last days of my mother's life trying to get her to accept Christ as her savior. Before the end, she said that she did accept Christ as her savior. Whether she said it just to shut Ralph up or not, is known to only one mortal, and she is dead.

When mom died, when she gave up the ghost, when she expired, whatever, the spirit of life fled. The sight was provocative. Anyone who has watched someone die is subject to being changed. To watch the color of life drain slowly from the skin. The osmosis of the wonder of life leaving the body is a terrible but wondrous thing. Life color slowly draining to ashen gray. Actually witnessing a body age ten years in ten minutes, like a bizarre episode of the Twilight Zone. Wrinkles appearing as if by magic. It's an amazing thing. Something has fled, not just expired. The thing lying on the bed is nearly unrecognizable. You do not recognize your own mother. That's a hard thing to understand. The subsequent death of my daughter was a different matter. I never once viewed the body. That whole thing was a mental puzzle, a grappling really. A study in the exasperating attempt to put some kind of value on death, some reason to keep you from becoming bitter, to understand why, when bullshit rains down on you in a deluge lasting years, why not take out your frustrations instead of looking for some mythical, elusive grace in a life that clearly holds only tribulation? Then, of course, if further study was needed, just in case I missed something the first two times, another ghost flies from my feet when my buddy drops dead. Another Twilight Zone episode.

My brother Ralph, in his imitable style, did his duty to his Christian savior and tried to save my soul. "Read the Bible asshole, what you got to lose? Your stupidity?" Well said. So I did, for my own imitable reason, because at this point in a man's life it was practical. I spend a lot of time in hotel rooms, on the road, doing my job, waiting. My job requires me to be on call seven days a week, twenty-four hours a day. When you live under these conditions you are susceptible to incredible boredom. I was fifty at this time; it's all downhill, physically from there. My job sometimes requires intense physical activity for an hour or two at a time. In between these hours of activity are days of inactivity. To save mind and body, I try to keep a simple regimen. Leave the TV off at least until 6pm, walk at least two miles a day and read as much as I can stand. For a time, reading the Bible was part of that regimen.

The Bible has been a source of inspiration, violence and debate for two thousand years. So what is the big deal? I set out to find out. I read it cover to cover in the King James version. It's too bad this book doesn't come with an artificial intelligence that you can plug in that would impart the essence of those many words. The text is a jumble of symbolism and innuendo coupled with an incredibly complex story line. It's a lot like trying to read Shakespeare. In short, the words, as they are written, take such a mental effort to decode, that most of the meaning flies right by me, hopefully to impact somewhere in my subliminal cortex. But I persevered. I had always been averse to reading one of the modern versions of the Bible. What are you getting? Clergy are just politicians in seek of your soul. I distrust politicians. But I relented. I then read the three hundred sixty-five day Bible, which splits the text of the old and new testaments up into three hundred sixty-five daily readings. But it is an interpretation by somebody. Is it accurate? Who knows? I suppose that if you buy into the idea that an omnipotent being can save your soul, you necessarily have to believe that if he really wants yours, he'll find a way to get a shot at it. Hence, modern version for modern man, translated by a spiritual medium, in this case, International Bible Society. What did I find in my quest for the essence of the Word? The leap of faith is the thing. Without the leap, no dice. I use the word "Leap" as a noun. It is an event, not an action. Until you experience the Leap, you are left in the dark. And it is kind of a chicken and egg thing, the leap and faith. So, I read my Bible, I walked my two miles and left the TV off.

God cannot be a being who occupies space and looks like a person. God must be an elemental part of the universe, a force, and the intelligence that guided creation. God must be a synapse-like life force, a charge of elemental energy that infuses that thing we call the soul with the basic elements of creation. I truly believe that that life-force/energy, synapse transcends mortal life. That initial mystical/spirituality/god-thing is a part of that which is called "heaven." It is part of us through our mortal life and transcends death to become again part of that thing called heaven, the soul. The Bible is a creation of man. I think that Moses not only hewed those stone tablets, I think he carved them, not once but both times. The undeniable force that existed in his soul was merely a broadcast agent for this unsophisticated man. He felt it, knew what it was and used the name given by his forefathers. This spiritual intelligence, this God. Moses was a genius in the spiritual sense. His genius brought him so close to that spiritual nature that exists in all of us, that he could actually commune with it. The way Mozart could commune with music. His genius embedded him right into the core of that living thing. The God he felt within him was so intense that, yeah, he did see it. Who is to say what are dreams and hallucinations? Did Mozart's mind's eye actually perceive the music before he wrote it down? Why Ten Commandments? What better way for Moses to impart spiritual wisdom than to distill it into something for the common man? Crime and Punishment. Things anybody can understand.

Poor reader. You now find yourself traveling through the littered and fevered mind of a hillbilly, talking about demons, Mozart and Moses. Led by whom? The hillbilly. The situation you find yourself in now is similar to the one I found myself in years ago. Books. Who is this hillbilly anyway, what does he really want? How many kids have found idealism in just this way? How many have found half-truths and how many have been taken off the real track? Traveling along in a book with someone who, for one reason or another, has gotten their attention. And if you are traveling in the back hills with a hillbilly in territory unfamiliar to you, what have you really got to guide you? Proceed from here at your own risk. But back to Moses.

Let's look at Moses from the fevered mind of a hillbilly. For over three thousand years the power of the human mind has been consistent. The power of the intellect has been consistent. What has changed is the huge pile of facts and information that have been compiled from that time until this time. The ability of a human mind to reason was just as potent in those days as it is now. But now we have the advantage of three thousand years of wisdom as a starting point. Wisdom and science -- facts. Moses was a genius. In my way of thinking geniuses are those empowered with the ability to transcend structured provincial, conventional thinking. Instead of memorizing dogma or facts, these geniuses among us somehow allow their minds to soar above and beyond all these facts and survey uncharted territory, using the facts as a rough road map.

In modern times, the vast arrays of technologies allow the geniuses of our times many avenues to travel. In ancient times these technologies were not available, so the great thinkers of those days focused on the things available to them. Philosophy doubled as science in those days. Along with philosophy was religion. Religion was a venue that was wide-open to a genius. Moses was a genius and he unleashed that genius on the venue of religion. Or maybe he was more comfortable with the word "spirituality," however that translates in Hebrew. He focused his mind on a venue available to him. Spirituality and the cause and effects of things. Some sort of God exists. Who can deny it? We have the same element in our body that exists in the sun -- hydrogen. We are of the sun. The sun exists due to a natural chemical reaction. Nature demands that fusion occur. Nature demands that fusion exists, and one of the reasons is so that light can shine on our planet and photosynthesis can occur. So on and so on. All of this just an accident of the cosmos and nature? What are the odds?

I think that Moses was over three thousand years closer to the event that sparked the creation of the sun. I think that the event that sparked the creation of the sun is the same event that planted part of the sun in each of us. I don't think that that was a haphazard event. Moses knew nothing of hydrogen atoms. His intellect was far more unfiltered, unadulterated than ours. His intellect was probably on par with Einstein or Hawking. His intellect was hooked on to the main line to the creation, unfiltered by centuries of conflicting theory.

The entire power of the genius Moses was focused on divining the essence of God. He was obsessed by that quest and he got closer to God than any of us ever will, at least in our mortality. He knew that he had to try to impart that essence, knew that he would fail with the masses. He was not armed with three thousand years of wisdom or facts, but he was closer to the event and the nature of the event and he was smarter than most of us. He knew. He also knew that he could never impart that knowledge. So he cloaked it in the Ten Commandments.

Moses had to settle for good and evil. But he and the other geniuses of the Old Testament laid bare their souls in a way that has lived through the ages. The scriptures, I believe, are a novelized form of how they achieved the wisdom of divinity through insights and visions so intense, so unfiltered, that they were rationally inexplicable. But the intensity of those insights was a mandate. When you are dealing in mandates that are pure knowledge assimilated through the genius of one individual, then you must resort to parable, acts of God and visions. The words to describe the actual thought do not exist. Our modern day challenge is to place ourselves in that place and time and try to unravel those events based on the ambiance of that time. I think that the interpreters of the Scriptures have planted the idea of a man-like God in our head. I think that Moses knew better. A lot of what I have said above is my gleanings from Mr. Pirsig's book.

Genius as defined by Webster, "extraordinary power of intellect, imagination or invention." Do you want to feel really stupid? Read a book called *The Elegant Universe*. It is about the current and most accepted theories of fundamental matter and the creation of the universe. (I wrote these words fifteen years ago, so whatever has happened in the scientific community may have advanced beyond the theories in this book). It tells, stepping-stone style, how the most brilliant minds of physics are trying to wed the two great branches of physics, general relativity and quantum mechanics, to explain how the universe was created and how it works. These guys are the ones who refute some of Einstein's theories. The book's author, Brian Green, is evidently one of the guys on the leading edge of these theories. He painstakingly, like a teacher to a first grade class, tries to distill and explain in layman's terms, how this all works. So, if you want to feel like an imbecilic first grader, take a shot at the book. Only in the broadest definition of the word, did I get it. These theories are so advanced and so complex and require such obscure flights of imagination, that my sad mental powers simply could not grasp them.

Okay, now we've got Moses, who is the spiritual genius of his time, the spiritual equivalent of Einstein or Newton. He alone grasps the complexity of the nature of his God. He is coming up from the other side, is going to meet Einstein in the middle, at the core of this thing. He had taken the leap; the wonders of God are then made known to him. The Leap. Now he has to explain it to guys like me and convince them to follow him around in the desert for forty years. Much better to give them something they can understand like crime and punishment, sin and virtue. Ah, why not give them Ten Commandments? The idea is to reach a point, at a level you can understand, where you too can be one with the true nature of yourself and your universe. God did write those stone tablets, with Moses hands as a medium. People like me have to, at some point in time, surrender to the natural order of things, understand that your puny intelligence is a grain of sand on an infinite beach and the only hope you ever have of understanding anything is after you're dead, maybe.

Does God evolve to keep pace with the dynamics of man and his society? Some people think so. The Universe is ever retreating and expanding, that's the theory. The really bizarre thing about the book *The Elegant Universe* is the belief now that the most basic particle, the core of all things, is not a particle at all but a vibrating string that emits energy in the form of wave patterns that dictate the creation of the basic building blocks of life. So the most basic ingredient in life is not an acid, not an atom, not a quark, but simply a life force, an energy. A synapse from God's brain maybe. The so-called "string theory."

So what about Jesus? Jesus is the son of Man, the son of God? Jesus, John the Baptist, Moses, etc. All spiritual geniuses. Manna from Heaven, the resurrection, all the other miracles? What of revelations? Unless you are a genius on par with Newton, Einstein, Moses or Jesus, it's unexplainable. You simply wouldn't understand. Anybody who is older than ten years knows that there is a censor in each of us. That censor dictates what is right and wrong. It can't be taught, it is just there. All of the scriptures are simply telling you to obey that censor, be true to yourself. There are those who do not possess that censor -- psychopaths and the like. Evil. But for those who do possess a censor, you must be true to that censor -- don't sin. Those who put themselves before their censor, before their true nature, before their God? Beware.

While I'm on the subject of geniuses, I find it fascinating to contemplate those who are known to possess genius. Genius -- what is it? I think it is merely the ability to have great insight and fly in the face of convention, when convention is wrong. The bold, guided step into virgin territory. Art, Science, Business, Religion. Pick your media. The act of genius is simply leaving conventional thinking behind and plunging headlong into the mystery of the unknown with confidence. The question is what is the thing that guides genius? What is the mental impetus that propels free thinkers on their quest? Where does it come from, that impetus that forces an exceptional talent along its path? God may love his flock, but it seems to me that he reserves his earth-shattering accomplishments for his freaks, his geniuses. The lightening of genius is not bestowed on the Martha Stewarts, but is saved for mainly freaks. John the Baptist, Moses, Jesus, Van Gogh, Einstein, Mozart, Steve Jobs, in my mind all freaks. People who defy convention, in fact, blast convention and conformity to smithereens. They follow their head, they have their own Way, and it is guided by the heart. Who of us has not had our finest moments when we left caution behind and let our heart take hold the reins of our mental ambition? Who has ever had their most satisfying moment following the demands of others?

The ecstasy of soul is heart-driven. As simple a thing as a bike helmet, somehow for me, is like a chain nailed to the wall of convention.

I have several flaws that have caused my problems over the years. One of these surfaced about the time of my twenty-fifth birthday. I had the delusion that I was an intellectual. The idea that all things could be dissected, analyzed and thoroughly understood by applying this huge intellect to bear on any question, it would necessarily provide logical conclusions. When you are twenty-five your belly doesn't sag, girls look at you with interest, you can drink all night and work all day, then do it again. The only thing of significance you have ever lost is your virginity. You've got forty years to worry about retirement, but most of all, as John Denver put it, "He was born in the summer of his twenty-seventh year." All of a sudden, being a man of the world, it seemed that I could do no wrong, me somehow being blessed with impunity to bad luck. My mom told me once that when I was born I had two placentas protecting me and that was the sign of a special baby. And I believed it. My recent stint in Africa had exposed me to that first fascinating glimpse of intelligent people who read a lot, talked a lot and had the money and opportunity to see and do extraordinary things. Long conversations with experienced people had given me a self-confidence in myself and my ideas. I prided myself on reading a variety of books on a spectrum of subjects. At the time I was smart enough to be able to devour a book in a couple of days, seemingly allowing the wisdom of those tomes to soak into my consciousness and shape my character in wonderful ways. I could discern the truth and come away changed and improved.

In this glowing light of self-importance, I found myself one day on an airplane bound for somewhere. I held in my hand a copy of *Time Magazine* that listed its picks for the ten best books of the year. One of those books caught my eye purely through the outrageousness of the title. *Zen and the Art of Motorcycle Maintenance.* I read the blurb and it sounded interesting enough to give it a shot. I got the book and later read it during a drive down the Alcan Highway. I was driving by myself under no deadlines. I read the book in the shade of the Canadian Rockies, mountains being a symbolic device for the author as well as John Denver and Moses too. I came away from that book with no real answers about God or the soul or anything else really. What I came away with was a unique way to look at these things, unique to me anyhow. And so for the next twenty-five years, I put religious questions on hold, pending further review.

So now, those twenty-five years later, after having left God back at Wrangell, I decided to revisit this book and see about some of that magic of twenty-five years ago. If I was now hell-bent on finding my spirituality, that seemed a good starting point, but cast now in the shadow of daily readings of King James. *Zen and the Art of Motorcycle Maintenance* is the story of a man running down the back trail of his own insanity on a motorcycle. He is traveling from the Midwest to the Pacific Ocean with his young son riding behind him. It is a true story, much in the same way that what I'm writing is a true story. What I am saying in this book is mostly true. The exact chronological order of some of the events is not accurate. I infer a lot about other people's thoughts and I have glazed over troublesome facts and emotions, and maybe just maybe, my personal biases have served me better than they should. But the effort is to present the truth as I remember it, and allow the reader to observe things that I alone have seen. But most important, the effort is to allow the reader to be a hitchhiker in the backseat of my personal mental vehicle. He is welcome to get out whenever he wants.

But, back to the book. The author, Robert Pirsig was a borderline genius, having the IQ of the top tenth of the top one percent of the general population. But as young prodigies will, he is dissatisfied with a lot that was being pushed at him as education. So he sets out to find the truth. This truth he calls "Quality," and as near as I can figure, this Quality is the spiritual God-force that kind of guides or predetermines those things in the Universe that have value, a.k.a. virtue. The problem is that his pursuit of this elusive Quality puts him at odds with just about everything in his life, and eventually he descends into a kind of depression that evolves into clinical insanity. The cure, shock treatment, reunites him with the world of everyday society but leaves great gaps in his memory. He is using this cross-country trip to retrace some of the places that he had lived before, trying to fill in the blanks in his memory and reconcile his insanity, for both him and his son. But through it all, he maintains this idea of Quality as a kind of twentieth century explanation for various great philosophical wisdoms of the past, both Eastern and Western. He ties the whole thing up with the rejection of some people in the late sixties and early seventies, of technology. Kind of the back to nature thing that was going on in those days. A truly fascinating book for a twenty-five year old kid who was full of himself, me.

It offered up some startling, to me, insights. Like demons. He says that ghosts or demons of the American Indian were real. Real in the sense that given the lack of technological data in those days, there we no atoms, no photons, no quarks, to help explain things. When the phenomenon you need to explain certain things has not yet been discovered, then you must make use of your present day vocabulary to explain things. Hence ghosts, visions, demons etc. Did gravity exist before Newton? Did Newton discover gravity, or just understand it well enough to give it a name and explain it to other people? The technology finally caught up with the phenomenon. When these types of people die, their discoveries do not. Today, our common sense is no more than a compilation of ghosts of the past. The people who made these great discoveries are all gone, but their ghosts remain and are quoted in books of history, mathematics and philosophy. The ghosts of Newton, Lincoln, and Socrates now inhabit our brains. We call them common sense. What once was magic is now common sense. So says Mister Pirsig.

He then goes on to break down the thought process into two distinct classes. Classical thought and Romantic thought and uses a motorcycle as an example. A classical mind will look at that motorcycle and see an array of moving valves, pistons, wheels, gases, etc., harmoniously combined to form a vehicle useful for transport, the vital part being the vehicle. The romantic will look at that same vehicle and see a method for getting into the wind at one hundred miles an hour so as to experience the rush. The vital part being the rush. Both people are right in their description of a motorcycle. The only real question being, what force guided the classical mind to the vision to provide the romantic mind with its means to achieve its experience, and how are the two wedded?

He then takes this premise and moves it into the realm of standard forms of spirituality. He uses the mountains symbolically. Moses climbed the mountains to attain enlightenment from God. He cites similar instances in Zen literature. He alludes to the Bible as a guide to ascend these mountains of enlightenment for those content to be guided. For those adventurous few, go seek at your own risk and you may find a path all your own, in which case you will be rewarded with a unique awareness. But beware, that awareness may cost you your sanity.

He then goes on to say that scientific truths, discovered over the last two thousand years are undermining the guided path of spirituality -- just try and part that Red Sea. Drop Moses or Jesus into the twentieth century, unidentified, speaking the same speeches they made centuries ago and they would both be remanded to mental institutions. Are the messages they brought to the world now untrue, or have the technologies and discoveries of two thousand years invalidated those messages by wiping out the scientific ignorance of those long ago places where the speeches were originally delivered? The God, or Quality, as Mr. Pirsig has named his ghost of the year 1976, would offer up his wisdom using different prophets, speaking in different symbolic terms, to describe the same truths. Will Durant said the same thing somewhat differently. "The Old Testament abounds in poetry and metaphor, the Jews who composed it did not take their own figures literally, but when European peoples, more literal and less imaginative, mistook these poems for science, our Occidental theology was born." Occidental roughly translates to "a mistake of the west." The fundamental truths are unchanged, the means to describe them are different and as always, mired in the unknown. Hence, you gotta have faith baby. But how do you keep the faith, baby?

Somehow the force, which he calls quality, others call God, is leading the way to some predestined end. At this point things start to get complicated. As it turns out, everyone reaches this point in his or her attempts to keep the faith baby. Mr. Persig's efforts take him to Jules Henri Poincare and threaten to lose me altogether. As near as I could follow it at the time, is that all people are infused with a certain harmony that is snatched out of the infinite number of chaotic possibilities, because this common harmony or Quality as he calls it, is really the hand of God guiding us along the path of truth. This hand of God leads all of us, if we choose to recognize it, to the one true end, through the labyrinth of possibilities that is the universe. Mr. Pirsig's Quality isn't the classical God, though they are one and the same, the difference being that the classical God of the Bible could only be understood in biblical days through the vernacular of those times. I'm not saying that this is what Pirsig meant, only what I understood him to mean, those twenty-five years ago.

From here he goes on to say that this quality is something that we all recognize, an internal sensor of good and bad, and if we live our lives by the mandates of this quality, if we care about our work and about our lives, that we are then doing the work of God, Quality, Buddha, or whatever your personal religion chooses to call this thing. But you must care, or you are part of the problem. This book contains almost four hundred pages and my summary here is only my gleaning of the essence as I saw it years ago. In the end, Pirsig ties up ideas of the Greek, Hindu and even Christian lines of reason, by showing how you can interchange words like Virtue and Dharma. I guess, at the time, I was as much in awe of the few crumbs I was able to glean as insight into the seemingly impregnable understanding of spirituality that had always eluded me.

So I started with this book. What I found twenty-five years later was something a little different. I read the book again and kind of the sequel to it that he published later. And so after rereading the book, I came to several conclusions. Again the conclusions are my own, not Pirsig's intent. First, Pirsig was just beating the brush around established Christian values, trying to put a spin on it that made sense to him. But his pathway to understanding was along the esoteric path of a loner intellectual. His attempt to define insanity as some sort of immaculate church of one, is valid I suppose, in the rarified air of the genius level intellectual. But what value did it have for little ol' me? I don't attempt to pass judgment on him -- I can't. He left me at about a 60% comprehension level of what he was trying to say. I only pass judgment on me for being arrogant enough to subscribe to his reasoning without truly understanding it. More importantly, for then arrogantly putting the real questions of faith on the shelf until further notice.

But it was a good place to start. So after finishing that book, I set out to look at other ideas. Along the way I revived past ideas, bastards conceived in books over the years, in conversations, in just listening to people, without, however, making a real commitment to any of them.

As good of a start as any is the idea that people in times of great stress actually descend into temporary insanity. My own mother alluded to something of the kind. I had the feeling many times that lack of sleep, too much alcohol, not eating right and the constant turning over of terrible thoughts in my mind, had made me delusional. At what point is delusion insanity? I have an old friend who is locked up for life. Twenty years ago he was one of the most competent people I knew. One day he had a seizure, then more. Within weeks he was unable to work. I didn't see him for ten years. He showed up one day looking for a job.

He showed me his driver's license like it was the Holy Grail. He regaled me with how the Lord has saved him at last. He regaled and regaled, lapsing into tedium. After a brief trial workday, I had to send him away. He was religious to the point of being disruptive. A week or so later, he took a hammer and killed three people who were staying at the same house as he. I am sure that he felt he was doing the work of the Lord.

My friend killed three innocent people because his brain had been altered. I found out later that doctors had cut out part of his brain. If you can render a man insane by cutting out part of his brain, can he also be rendered insane by taxing certain portions of that same brain through daily doses of alcohol and fatigue to the point of disease? Is the result insanity? If you don't know, how can you ever tell? Insanity, my definition. Deviant behavior or a different way of thinking. Perception from a viewpoint whose access is gained by a very few. That access is either actively sought, or the result of being washed up on the shore of that vantage point.

Or maybe Shirley McClain has the answer. She says that she has lived previous lives. Maybe there is something to that. My sister told me about a theory that one of her friends told her about. The idea that genes, along with conveying physical and mental traits, may also somehow allow memories of our ancestors to bleed into this transportation process. Maybe partial memories of ten previous generations are conveyed genetically to you. Maybe the thing we call conscience is just a warden to a prison full of ancestors who are trying to have one last hurrah. Ted Bundy, in his final days, talked of the killer within, as if he was referring to another person. William Styron in his book about depression, *Darkness Visible* said, "A phenomenon that a number of people have noted while in deep depression is the sense of being accompanied by a second self--a wraithlike observer who not sharing the dementia of the double, is able to watch with dispassionate curiosity as his companion struggles against oncoming disaster, or decides to embrace it." There is a killer buried in all of us, given the right provocation. Maybe there are other folks in there as well. And maybe those folks have brought some of their demons with them.

You see where this is going. How do you reconcile thoughts in your head, the events in your life with the grand idea of a spirituality, a kind of sanctuary where you can go for respite and find soothing thoughts, if your head is peopled with demons and spirits that might get awakened in the process?

If you hope that an eternity of spirituality is the reward for a life well lived, then the travails of this world are inconsequential. What then is Heaven? Hanging around with a bunch of beings that possess no vices? And Hell? What is the reality of the metaphorical eternal fire? What if that's just hype delivered by manipulative people who want your money and to keep you in line? What if this life is all you get? What about the possibility that the whole enchilada is the journey itself? Still, most people believe that no matter how hard the journey is, you must travel the journey with grace and good effort. When gloom lays on your days like a bad smell? A smell like a dead rat that you cannot find, no matter how hard you try. Then you begin to question the spiritual thing. This grace under fire thing. How about when this spiritual thing is a two hundred pound pack you carry, every day, uphill, with no blue sky in sight. Well, if that is the price you pay for spirituality, or if spirituality is just the journey itself, then what's the point in spirituality or the journey, when it is a lead foot-hike up a steep hill in the gloom? That necessarily takes you to the question posed by Albert Camus. "There is but one truly serious philosophical problem, and that is suicide. Judging whether life is or is not worth living amounts to answering the fundamental question of philosophy." Who wants to go there? But if you are an objective, logical person, you must go there. What then is that mental device that automatically submits a resounding no? And what if that device says, "Whatever"?

But let's say that the answer is no. So, the fear of death is truly more terrifying than carrying a dead two hundred pound rat around for the rest of your days. Your first clue then is that arrogant as you are, you are still not sure what happens when you die. Is that the first step in losing the Witch? Life sucks right now, but I'm just not ready for what happens next. Or are you being foolish and just playing into her hands. You've got to remember, somebody with no faith is someone with no cards in a game where the Witch is dealing. The Witch demands that you test Camus's theory if you have no faith.

Remember when I said that a good author has the ability of crystallizing vagrant thoughts in your head into mental images that strike a chord of truth? Why then, after several readings of the Bible in two different versions, is the process still like reading the James Joyce novel, *Ulysses*? Everyone proclaims that both of these masterpieces of literature are works of vision and knowledge. Not to me. Now why is that? If God can speak to people for two thousand years through this great book, why is it a brick wall for me? Keep hammering and move on.

Maybe money is the answer. Maybe if I can get enough money, happiness will cascade down on me like manna from heaven. The crux of the money matter boils down to a relatively simple idea. One that I can understand. The idea of success in this century in this country is coupled inexorably with the idea of money. But it seemed to me the pursuit of money is what landed me in this mess. The Bible of course is very clear on this point. A rich man has less chance of attaining heaven then a camel crawling through the eye of a needle. The idea of pursuing money still has me baffled to a point, but it is so necessary. I have come to a simple conclusion. It is how you pursue riches that matter. The riches themselves are a good as near as I can tell. The danger you run into in the pursuit of it, is emulating successful people in order to achieve it. People who have no resemblance to you.

Henry Miller: "Everyman has his own destiny, the only imperative is to follow it, accept it, where ever it leads." Or if you prefer scripture: Ecclesiastes 3:22, "Wherefore I perceive that there is nothing better, than that a man should rejoice in his own works, for that is his portion: for who shall bring him to see what shall be after him?" Do I really want to be rich if I have to be like Donald Trump? Or do I just want the keys to his bank account on my own terms. There are hundreds of motivational books and outlined recipes for success and, if the all-important goal is a certain amount of money, I think that goal is attainable for most folks. The problem is that you may lose your identity along the way and use up the days of your life in the process. So I decided to pursue the money, but not the bouffant hairdo of Donald Trump. If you never get where you are going, at least you can enjoy the trip.

My efforts in the pursuit of the big bucks have cost me greatly. I now believe I was paying the price for pursuing other people's dreams. Eyes wide open of course. In the end, I failed at most things, almost all things of importance. I failed as a husband. I failed as a father. I failed as a businessman. I failed as a pilot. I nearly failed marriage a second time. I could have failed as a parent a second time, might yet. I came close to failing at several friendships that were important to me. The list goes on and on. Part of the root to all these failures was the pursuit of money.

Maybe if you blame other people for your problems, you can save your self-esteem, which you must have to find your soul. Self-esteem, self-love. Blaming other people for your problems is a simple and righteous endeavor. Answers a lot of questions that maybe would better be left unasked. For example, if someone, in your eyes did you a wrong, this issue of self-esteem somehow is transferred into your own inability to deal with the dominance from another person or situation. Someone or something had power over you that you were unable to deal with equitably. You are left wanting, kicked in the ribs of your self-esteem. The situation of low self-esteem is simply admitting that someone or something has dominance over you to which you have no answer. The fact is that dominance by other people, more accurately, the attempt by other people to dominate you is just a fact of nature. Law of the jungle. To recognize this fact is not the same as to be defeated by it. There are those people in this society who have dominance over you. Starts with your parents, goes from there. The solution of course is to find a way to elevate yourself in some fashion, so as to confront these people or situations from a position of equality. Dominance, like any natural law, is a dynamic that is affected by many forces. The most important thing for the individual is to search for that quality, that power, that inspiration within oneself that can be a catalyst to achieve the end that you are searching for. For Martin Luther King, it was nonviolent protest. To Ray Charles, it was God's gift of music. I think that self-esteem, like your immune system, must be tested constantly to keep it strong. But if you are not happy in what you are doing, not striving for a goal of your own conception? Where does that leave you?

It appears to me that many of the dominant forces you confront in society live outside the rules of that society, or at least push at the borders. Some of these forces are malevolent in intent. Just ask an LA cop. Does self-interest ring a bell? Self-interest is the double- edged sword that swings like a pendulum among opposing forces. I have never been to a therapist. But unless they tell you that there are real assholes out there who want your money and will hurt you to get it if they have too, they are not addressing the whole problem. If they don't relate that simple fact, then they shift the fulcrum of the double-edged sword in favor or those forces that want to dominate you. Lifting your self-esteem is important, but not as important as discovering your relative strengths, accepting them, and finding a catalyst or alliance that will raise you, blemishes and all, to a level where you can neutralize those dominant forces. It's not vital to completely like yourself. It's much more important to accept who you are than to love who you are. The whole idea is that you must muster your resources as best you can and deal with life day to day. Abhorrent as it may be, Jeffrey Dahlmer is as much a part of nature as Jesus Christ, at least according to the philosopher, Henry Spencer. And dealing with that is so important. Here again you have to accept things you cannot change. Will Durant wrote, "Perhaps we shall someday be strong enough and clear enough in soul to see the shining beauty of even the darkest truth." Nature is often cruel and barbaric. But all of it, every last bit of it, is part of the whole that God created. We don't have to like it but we must accept it.

But all this was leading around in a circle, back to the primary question of Albert Camus. Suicide or no? Is life really meaningless? The joy, the pain, the ecstasy, the despair each individual experiences, are simply emotions nature invented to keep you interested in the journey. The real purpose being that each individual person is nothing more than an organic conveyor belt? Are we just a genetic conveyance from our parents to our children that nature uses in the ongoing refinement of the earth's dominant species? All this spiritual nonsense planted by crafty con artists who want to control us? Perpetuated by our fear of the dark? Is our entire Universe simply a quark in an atom of the Cosmos? One infinitesimally small, insignificant mote of matter in a cosmos so large that each individual counts less than an atom of a grain of sand in the Sahara?

But what of the incredible magic that is conscious thought. Again, just insignificant? Something that may soon be manufactured. Manufactured thought. The ability of mankind to conceive magical thoughts out of thin air and turn them into thinking machines? What happens when those machines are finally equipped with organic components that allow those same machines to make the first conceptual leap, leaving simple computations behind? Does that small mass of organic material, maybe mined from a human brain, then infuse that machine with a soul? Is a soul tethered somehow to conscious thought? Are stillborn or aborted babies soulless?

Going back to this grand conveyor theory. Maybe this grand, unending organic conveyor works inexorably toward that event called the Apocalypse. Each individual soul, when it is freed upon death, is deposited in that place called heaven where it takes its assigned place, generation after generation as we travel slave-like towards the great event. When that great event finally takes place, all the souls cemented in their assigned places now form a huge mosaic that, when seen from a distance, is the body of god. Or if you move father back, just the back door to the event called Geneses by some, the big bang by others. The mosaic being nothing more than fertile gases ready to explode into the next stage of this drama. Maybe creation is the sum of all souls, so-called heaven, and depending on your beliefs, just gases for the next big bang or the clay for the Creator's next Genesis.

What's the answer? You gotta have faith baby. Because if you use your intellect as a divining rod in things spiritual, you run great risks. Romans 1:18 through 23: "For the wrath of God is revealed from heaven against all ungodliness and unrighteousness of men, who hold the truth in unrighteousness; Because that which may be known of God is manifest in them; for God hath shewed it unto them. For the invisible things of him form creation of the world are clearly seen, being understood by the things that are made, even his eternal power and Godhead: so that they are without excuse: because that, when they knew God, they glorified him not as God, neither were thankful; but became vain in their imaginations, and their foolish heart was darkened. Professing themselves to be wise, they became fools, and changed the glory of the uncorruptible God into an image made like to be corruptible man, and to birds, and fourfooted beasts, and creeping things." The world around you is enough evidence to know that God exists, to think otherwise is cause for damnation. To think that you can figure out what God is, that effort makes you a fool, because you are limited by your intelligence. God is not. You gotta have faith baby. And I suppose that the world around you is the best argument.

Chapter VII
SOME ANSWERS

St. Mark 9:25: "Thou dumb and deaf spirit, I charge thee, come out of him, and enter no more into him"

Wˑhen my wife isn't calling me worst-case scenario, she calls me unkempt Ned. Ned being a nickname from my youth. I am kind of a messy person and often leave doors open, dishes on the sink, things left undone. So it was that I left my search for spirituality unfinished. Instead, taking God's warning to heart, I got to thinking more and more about the Incident. The winter expired into spring and finally summer. I decided to revisit the incident. I have played a little trick on the reader. Earlier in this book I mentioned an incident where Becky and I went dip netting at the Copper River, and I fell in and ruined the whole day. Unless you have ever seen the Copper River you would not know that you don't just fall in the Copper River. To fall into the Copper River is to put your life at risk.

When the next summer had arrived and the salmon were again running in the Copper River, I took my dip net and I returned. I chose to go alone. I suppose I wanted to be alone. You can never be alone on the Copper River though. It has a presence all its own. To believe that there are no absolute truths in life is to exclude that great river from your experience.

The Copper River is the absolute Truth. This river is a catastrophic grinder. For hundreds of miles it tears at its bank. It carries away soil, it chips at the rock. Glaciers feed it with ancient ice. Released from that ice is the flora and fauna of the ages. Flooded tributary creeks contribute whole trees and debris of every description. The great river is perpetually chewing up terra firma and sending it piecemeal into Prince William

Sound. The great natural irony is that hidden beneath the impenetrable surface of the silt-laden conveyor, is one of the world's great salmon nurseries. While the river is busy at slowly ripping away the earth that lines its banks, it is a nursery for one of the premier salmon runs in the world. Beneath the boiling surface, millions of salmon work their way upstream in the last stages of their timeless journey. Starting in May, the Kings, or Chinook. In mid-June, the Sockeye or Red's. Then in August the Coho, or Silver. Those fish are driven upriver to the tributary of their birth, there to lay or fertilize eggs, then donate their soft red flesh to the bear, the eagle, and the trout. It's a mystery and it's the Truth.

I found my sweet spot, my not so secret spot. It was a weekday and I was lucky to have the place to myself. I wasn't really all that interested in fishing. I just wanted to be here and think things over. Wearing tennis shoes, I had worked my way down the steep face of the talus slope and had reached the river uneventfully. The fact that there were not many fish that day was OK: they would just have been a nuisance. I did manage to net about five fish. Having spent a couple of hours holding the long-handled net in the rushing current for that period of time, I had a sore back and was in need of a beer.

Later, the fish were on ice. I decided that I would call it a day. I pulled the bottle of Beam from my duffle bag and poured a generous shot into my coffee cup. I intended to sleep in my truck and start home whenever I woke up. I sat on the hood of my truck. The pull-off, on the narrow winding road that follows the west bank of the river, gave me a good view of the river in both directions. I was on a promontory maybe three hundred feet above the river. I sat facing upriver. The noise. The constant, muted roaring of the river was so pervasive, it became silent after a time, more a part of the visual image, than a soundtrack for it. The river is the color of the mud that drains from your truck when you wash it after four days of 4-wheeling in Western Washington, if you then mixed that mud with milk. The many glaciers draining into this river give it a translucent, milky appearance.

The river narrows here. There are three tree-lined layers of ridges running in from my left. The farthest is the dark, emerald green of mostly spruce. Here and there, escarpments of gray granite give gnarly teeth to the face of this ridge. The middle ridge is multicolored. The emerald of the live spruce is peppered here and there with the frosty brown of beetle-killed spruce. Lush green of willows and aspen dot the ridge also, flashing the silver underside of windblown leaves. A single open scar of granite face mars the lush intermediate ridge. The near ridge, the one that falls at a sixty-degree angle to the water's edge is mostly just the broken and fallen scree of weathered shale. At the base of this ridge, fingers of layered rock grasp at the turgid brown water like the knuckles of a spread hand. Scattered among this talus, are small individual spruce and willows marching uphill in ragged single file.

The river is about three hundred feet wide here. The opposite bank is a face of sheer granite, reaching straight up to a height of one hundred feet. At the water line are colonies of ochre colored lichen or moss. Farther up, a solitary spruce has found enough nourishment to take root in a pocket of soil notched into the granite face. Willows have surrounded the lone evergreen, waiting patiently for the spruce beetles to finish their work. A green mass gives texture to the stark granite face. Purple lupine and white dots of some alpine flowers give it character.

An angry sky of soft-looking clouds has lowered onto the valley, giving the effect of a tunnel. The sky limits sight to the three, layered ridges, perhaps five miles. Peeking through, seven miles distant, is a blue ridge line, then just clouds. The whole thing is the river of course. The entire landscape pours down upon it to make it the focus. The river is lord and master here. All is the domain of the river.

I'm done fishing. In the glow of the amber liquid sluicing around in my coffee cup, I'm thinking about the incident and I'm thinking about all of those books. Forty years of books. Reading is another double-edged sword. You learn valuable things from books. In the realm of religion and philosophy though, the path is littered with footprints in all directions. As if a pack of wolves had descended on a herd of only juvenile caribou, in deep snow. Great carnage without a discernible pattern. Trails running off in every direction. The landscape is ripped and torn. Only a woodsman of great skill can read the story. And me, a city boy.

The job of education is a simple one. Educators are expected to equip their charges with the tools they need to discern the truth. Kids should be given the faculties so that they are able to discern the truth. Nothing more. For most of us, a lifetime is spent in the pursuit of the truth. The discernment of the truth. And how is this simple pursuit to be accomplished?

Karl Marx wrote a book on economics. Adam Smith wrote one as well. Only in the last twenty years has it been proven beyond a reasonable doubt that Smith's ideas are more valid than Marx's, at least for this period of history. But maybe that is only true for a brief period of time, maybe a hundred years of so. Hitler wrote a book called *Mein Kamph.* That book polarized a generation of Germans and propelled them to the precipice of world domination. But in the end, it didn't fly. Though millions of people were educated by that book, in the end, those millions had been misled and at a terrible cost. But that book was written to play on the emotions of the German people, Hitler was a master psychologist, and even the educated masses of the German people were led awry by tainted words. Ayn Rand wrote several books that some might construe to be in conflict with the one written by Al Gore, *Earth in the Balance.* Each of these books have scholars on both sides of the fence, deeply intelligent humans, stridently proclaiming the virtues of their particular champion. Rand seems to proclaim that man is the master, his legacy all-important, the earth is his canvas. I have not read Gore's book but have been told that his theme is that earth is the master, man custodian. How is a common guy with average intelligence supposed to sort it all out? Then of course, there is religion.

The river narrows here. Right in front of me, you can see where the broad, brooding river is forced into a venturi, gaining momentum. In the 1970's, I was young and was first introduced to conflicting ideas brought forth by a group of people with whom I worked. The diversity of these ideas was simply a representative of the spectrum of the group. The oldest attained adulthood during World War II, veterans some, from two of the allied powers. Deeply influenced by the great depression and staunchly patriotic. Then there were Korean War veterans, Cold War adults, slightly disillusioned by politics. Vietnam War veterans. This group was deeply disillusioned or merely apathetic and often in open conflict, politically, with the other veterans. Others of the same age during all three wars were civilians and spouses. On top of this were people from a wholly different society. There were some that represented the vestiges of Colonial Africa. Then, Africans themselves, black and white. Everybody had stories, books or both. And of course in the era of Vietnam, society in general was in upheaval. The legacy of World War II, Korea, Vietnam, the dismantling of Colonial Africa. Religion, politics, morality had so many faces that the landscape resembled a party at the

UN after a general session. Each and every participant knew the truth and they were selling it to you. Or maybe they just wanted your vote.

I sat for a time looking upriver. Up that way a couple of miles is a stretch of river that borders the main road. In June of 1982, I had first come to this river. My infant daughter was just two weeks old when her mother and I loaded up the old Ford and did a short tour of Alaska. I didn't net any fish that time, but it was one of only a dozen or so vacations I would spend with my daughter. Each of those has taken on more importance. It was a time in my life when anything was possible and the idea that a day would come when my happiness, and even my sanity would be in question, seemed as remote as the faraway approach of the new millennium. Both those things had arrived about the same time. Now this idea of rooting the Black Witch out of my life by somehow getting a spiritual ghost to chase her away, was wearing a little thin. But maybe I had learned something of value from all those books. Maybe the problem was simply how you thought about this elusive spirituality. Maybe if I took a little advice from that most holy of all Christian books and turned it over enough times, maybe an answer would fall out. Romans 1:20: "For the invisible things of him from creation of the world are clearly seen, being understood by the things that are made…." Well if God made that river down there, I was sure seeing it clearly. Maybe the message was in the river. Maybe the answer lay right down there in that roiling brown water. Maybe my great Deity was hidden beneath the glacial runoff somewhere there below my feet.

The river narrows here. When I turn around and take a sip of bourbon, I am now facing downriver. From here you can see where the canyon funnels the river into an even more narrow section. The flow of the river becomes a malevolent torrent. Kind of a lateral avalanche of water that tears and churns through the cut face of the canyon. There are huge waves here that buck and writhe over unseen obstacles below the surface. I'm looking for the spot. I am uncertain because I last approached it by boat at water level. An entirely different perspective than the one from this vantage point. It doesn't matter much. The fact was that the charter boat operator had set me on a good-looking eddy on the far side of the river. I had come for meat that day. That day of a year ago.

It had not been going well that day. Becky and I had come in our old motorhome and had camped on the windswept beach at O'Brien

Creek. And of course the Black Witch had been at work that day. Becky was suffering from an attack of her arthritis. Weather changes often bring on a severe attack, and so it was on that day. Her spirits were low. It was only a couple of weeks after Billy's death. My mood was foul, nursing a hangover, no doubt. The wind was blowing hard. Becky decided that she just couldn't come with me. I probably would have just as soon forgotten the whole thing, but I had made a commitment with the charter boat operator. So I went ahead, alone. For some reason I had my hip waders on and was carrying my tennis shoes and some other things in a garbage bag. I probably figured I might get wet getting out of the boat.

Later, I had sat in the boat on the trip downriver with the other paying customers, and for a while the river was the only thing. The river has its way here. The mountains on either side stand like mute, eunuch sentinels, powerless witness to this great mother of destruction. No matter what my mood, I always sat in reverence when I watched this river. We went downriver from O'Brien Creek. I was sitting in the back of the jet boat and was under siege of the roaring of the engine. It didn't matter. The river is alive like a mortally wounded animal is alive. It's like it is in the last stages of living. When all energy is focused on just staying alive. It was writhing and kicking and screaming. A living thing, expending all its energy in its death throes. An eternity of death throes. A magnificent sight.

I was dropped off at a dome-like rock about twenty feet across, in the shape of a crescent moon, the convex rounded part shoring the river. The upstream portion of the rock worked the current into an intermittent eddy. An eddy is a term used to describe a portion of the river that actually flows upstream, in conflict with the normal flow. The action of the river striking the rounded protuberance of the rock worked in two ways. For long moments, the jutting, rounded edge of the rock served only to sweep the current around its face and then backed into an eddy on the downstream side of the rock. Without warning, and without any regularity or cadence, the current would change and suddenly the upriver portion of the rock would become the fulcrum for the water to reverse direction and momentarily flow upriver, against the normal flow, thereby forming a temporary eddy. When this eddy action was activated, you simply stuck your net into the water and the contrary flow of the river would string out the net in the water, forming a perfect trap for the fish swimming upriver. This method was much less tiring than sweeping the net downriver to create the same effect. In minutes, that constant sweeping motion works mercilessly at the muscles in your arms, lower back and legs. The dueling eddies that were on either side of me always provided me a place for my net. When one side of the rock was eddying, so to speak, the other side was sweeping downriver with the current. So I worked first one and then the other.

The river was a torrent here, moving at perhaps fifteen miles an hour, and turbulent. Twenty feet out from where I stood, the water was in all-out assault, surging downriver amidst the swelling and roiling wave action. The cascading water was splashing the face of my rock, keeping it wet. I tested the surface of the rock with my waders. There was a gritty grain and it seemed secure enough. I decided to keep the waders on and have dry feet. Many people who work the river with nets use a harness to lash themselves to a deadman -- a secure place to tie off your rope. A rock or tree usually serves this purpose. The common method is to adjust the tether, a nylon rope in most cases, so at maximum length the harness keeps the dip netter just short of the water's edge. Should the dip netter lose his footing, the rope will keep him out of the water. I had always distained this setup as cumbersome and unnecessary.

I had begun by working the upstream eddy. I would stick my net into the eddy when the river was working that way. When the eddy disappeared, I would just wait until it returned. I was in no hurry. I had all day. It was windy on that day, but bright, clear skies were an awesome spectacle. But I wasn't getting any fish. I moved to the downstream eddy then. Working this eddy gave me a view of the river downstream. I could see a couple of dip netters about two hundred yards from me. They had been dropped off on at a rock that was sticking farther out into the main current than my position. I watched them as they landed fish after fish. My mood had been improving to this point, but as I watched them hammer the fish and me getting nothing, my mood turned back south. Normally, getting no fish doesn't bother me much. I really come to be here, on the Copper River. The fish are just a bonus. But today, I had paid $100.00 to the charter boat guy and I wanted fish. The river was not an inspiring muse, not today. Today it was a fish market. I was here for meat. So I began to sweep. I simply decided that by the force of my will, I would sweep that damn river until I had at least fifteen fish. And I began to get results.

Steve Scott

A dip net is a net about three feet in diameter. It is attached to a pole anywhere from four feet to twenty feet long. The one I had was made of aluminum. It had been supplied by the charter boat operator. It was about fifteen feet long I suppose. I was at the water's edge. I would plunge the net into the water at about a sixty-degree upstream angle and sweep it down with the current, the idea being to keep the net splayed out so as to provide an opening for the fish to swim into. When a fish hits, it feels like a slight bump if you feel it at all. The idea then, is to rotate the pole ninety degrees, thus closing the net around the fish as you simultaneously raise the net out of the water, hopefully with the fish still inside. Sweeping is hard work but generally you get better results than just sticking your net into an eddy and waiting. I had about five fish on the bank and all of a sudden nothing. I swept steady for half an hour and still nothing. I sat down to take a rest. My back was starting to tighten up a bit. While I was sitting, I watched the couple up river land a big one. Must have been a King, a Chinook. That did it. I got back up and really started in again. It was a test between me and the fish now. I would get the goddamned fish if I wrecked my back in the process.

I was talking to myself now. Goddamned fish, goddamned river. I was in the middle of a sweep, really leaning into it, when my right foot just let go. I pirouetted off my left foot, perfectly balanced, six inches from the water's edge. The net! The weight of the net tipped my balancing act. I donated it to the river but it was too late. I don't remember going into the water. I remember being in the water. I remember surfacing. I came up blowing water like a sounding whale. My first sensation was of my hip waders filling with water. I came up facing the boiling expanse, the opposite shore obscured by the broiling torrent in front of me. I said the words aloud, didn't shout, "Don't panic." I spun around to face the shore. I was about two feet from the rock. No bottom could I feel. I had gone into the river at the point of the extreme upstream part of the rock. The river now swept me along the face of the rock. I reached out to grab something, but there was only rock. My hands slid along the slick surface like they were greased, the rock a baby's butt. I just slid on by. At that moment the flood gates opened, adrenalin coursed into my veins. In an instant I was stoned. The adrenalin rush.

The true adrenaline rush. How many times in my life had I felt that my life was in immediate peril? Counting this time, I would say five. Maybe three or four other times when there was more than a little concern. Then the time I got into a real fight and the two times my airplane engine sputtered. We're not talking the high you get in controlled situations, like going fast on a motorcycle. Just the times that the situation was not in control and you wanted out. Out of the fifty years of my life, adrenalin had flowed un-summoned into my blood in a life-threatening situation, maybe five times. How long did it take to sweep down the face of that rock? So in the span of three or four seconds my desperate hands found no solace, and adrenaline rushed through a floodgate and into my bloodstream.

Adrenalin -- what's it feel like? The strange thing about it, is that it always seems to address the nature of the immediate threat. The time I was getting the shit beat out of me, it eliminated all pain. The time I hit the train, instantaneous reactions. The time I was doing about a hundred and ten and the guy I was about to pass made a left turn in front of me, dead calm. The time in the Hercules, when we broke out of a solid cloudbank to find ourselves surrounded by mountains on all sides and me helpless, standing behind three pilot? It was like I was a casual viewer at a movie theater who had just been given a slug of morphine. This day, when I was a piece of flotsam being swept downriver, I thought I might live to be two thousand years old, for the euphoria in my head, clearness of my brain. The only words spoken were, "don't panic". Somehow the functions of my brain were broken down into at least five different areas. One was focusing on my hands, another on my filling boots, another on my options, still another musing on the ridiculousness of my situation, seeing humor there. That my life was in peril was beyond question. Ten seconds would decide the issue.

The river swept me along the entire length of the rock. My back was to the river, I was trying mightily to find something to grab onto. Then the rock was gone. I was in the river. I was done. At that precise instant, time stopped. My little brain went into overdrive and I felt oh so fine, immortal. Adrenalin may be better than sex. No more decisions, now it was all about how long could I battle the river, just the physical now. My boots were half full; the boiling river was my attention. Just stay afloat! Then, unbelievably, I stopped! I stopped right in the teeth of the current. I was in the eye of the hurricane. I was suddenly caught in a forming eddy. I could reach my hand out if I wanted too, take some handfuls of rushing current and be shot downriver to certain doom. Not three feet away the river was plunging headlong downstream at fifteen miles an hour. Where I was, it was motionless. My thoughts were out of control. Buttons were being pushed. Emotions flashed around like lightening. I was merely a bystander. An observer, stoned to a state of perfect lucidity. Just watching to see what would happen next.

Then it started backing up. *The river started backing up.* The river pushed me back along the entire face of the rock. Still I could grab nothing. Another ten seconds. Finally, when the eddy stopped at its upstream zenith, I grabbed a handhold. The quart of adrenaline was now focused on a handhold the size of a sand dollar. As the force of the eddy died and started to waft back downstream, I took my shot. I pulled with everything I had and the sand dollar held. I was chest out now. One boot tore loose. Focusing all of me on my right hand, I pulled up and sat my fat ass on the shelf of the twenty-foot rock.

Man did I feel good. I wish I had a six-pack of that adrenalin stuff. I sat there and started laughing. But it was sixty degrees out and the wind was blowing and I was soaking wet. Pretty soon I was shaking, shaking with laughter and something else. I peeled the other boot off and hurled it into the slashing water. It was gone in an instant. I was really shaking now. I carefully sloshed up the face of the rock and onto real dirt. I went to my garbage bag and got out dry socks and tennis shoes. I peeled off my soaked shirt and put on my jacket, then dry socks and shoes. I had about four hours before the charter guys would come and get me. So I sat for a time. I was surprised at how quickly the wind dried my drenched pants. I was dry and comfortable in less than an hour. There was nothing to do but wait. My dip net was probably closer to Cordova than here to me by now. I had five dead fish to deal with, so I did that.

I had brought a filet knife with me. I found a reasonably flat portion of rock and started filleting fish. After I finished the first fish, I was about to throw the carcass in the river, but somehow I was now surrounded by about twenty squawking seagulls. I launched the carcass up onto the bank and three gulls were on it immediately. The big guy won, and perching on a rock, went immediately after the eyeballs. The next fish was a female. I threw the eggs one way and the carcass another. The big guy didn't hesitate. He was on the eggs when they landed. Three other gulls had the carcass. Same story; eyes first, then the carcass. It seemed the gulls had their priorities. Eggs, eyes, and then the rest. I finished the fish, the gulls left after dinner, and I was alone. The seagulls had their priorities. Maybe it was about time to name some of my own.

I sat there and I thought about my daughter. My dead daughter. The roaring of the river provided a muted symphony of exquisite elegance. The view from my rock would be a perfect portal to heaven. There was no better place in God's creation to do this. To think of my daughter with the hangover of an euphoric drug still giving me little stabs of emotion.

Interlude with Sherry, part seven

"Starry, starry night. Flaming flowers that brightly blaze..." Don McLean

I am sitting on the bank of the once great Colorado River. We are done for the day. My back hurts like hell. I was one of the "bow blasters" on our three man raft. The Marquita in my hand truly is a blessing on this day. The setting sun was turning the shades of the Grand Canyon into a pastel colored paradox. The bright colors of the mid-day sun had been muted. The canyon walls were being bathed in a peaceful dying ochre. Soon the blanket of the ages would start popping out stabs of light from the heavens. From a tent a couple hundred feet away I could hear a moaning, rising in timbre and calling out my name. Sherry...Sherry. The guy was drunk.

I had put on some muscle in the last couple weeks. Running the river for days on end, paddling a lot of the way, I had gotten into pretty good shape. I had come up on shore in front of him. My tank top was soaked from the last set of rapids. I had bent over the raft and looked up to see him staring at me. Well, staring at the water soaked tank top. I wore no bra. I guess I still looked pretty good. Tasha had been dead for three years. I was on one of the best trips of my life. It was starting to make sense again. The world. Tasha not in it. Get over it? Never happen. I wasn't pitching the tent tonight. I would sleep out under the stars. I would dream of Tasha, but I would sleep soundly. The stars, you could almost hear them. Like you heard the Northern Lights those many years ago, when I held her close, those lights reflecting in baby Tasha's eyes as she pointed at that Aurora when she was only three. She had pointed at those lights and laughed with the untroubled joy of one so young. Shit, my throat was constricting. I would be crying soon. I just lay down on my sleeping bag, let the tears come and stared up at the stars, now blinking, now afire, now ablaze. She would come to me tonight, my Tasha.

And now, one year later, I thought of her again. The task of taking mental images and forming those images into a living, breathing beauty is the most formidable emotional exercise that I had ever had to perform. Now that breathing beauty was not breathing anywhere except in a hallowed portion of a mostly used up brain. I had done my part in killing that beauty. I had let that exquisite beauty get out of my sphere of influence. I had driven her and her mom and her brother out of my life. That fact was unchangeable. No act of God could change that. I could not change it. I could only live with it. To hell with preachers, to hell with friends and family, to hell with the Black Witch. My life was changed. Nothing could help me or change that one simple fact. My daughter lay six feet under the living, breathing air. She lay in a black sepulcher enfolded in the grip of black earth. I had had a hand in that. The best part I had to offer to the world was gone, irretrievable. I had to learn to deal with that or I would perish, and both me and my daughter would be defeated. It did matter. Our lives did matter, God damn it.

Some things are sacred. Very few things. My personal thoughts about my daughter are one of these. It's a place where words do not exist. It's a place where the heart doesn't pump blood. It's a place where the heart pumps the pure emotion that cannot exist anywhere but the source of that pump. The great secret of the universe is entombed somewhere in the heart. The soul is not any part of the brain, so words do not exist there. The brain is like a eunuch sentinel. It can watch and observe, protect the soul or maybe, try to. But the brain is impotent in matters of the soul. The secret of the universe courses wordlessly through our ephemeral mortality. When we die, the secret dies with us, at least for this world of mortals. The Bible is mortal man's attempt to corral that secret. But it will not be corralled. The secret has been planted into each of us. Our five perceptive senses are blue-light flashbulbs fired at irregular intervals. Our natural world is like tapestry hung on an infinite wall. Embedded in that tapestry is the truth of the Great Secret. In an incredibly complex mosaic are the elements of that truth that are lit up by that blue-light strobe of our intelligence. Unfortunately, that part of the tapestry that is illuminated by the blue light is but an infinitely tiny part of the whole mosaic. An infinitely small part of the secret mosaic is visible only during the flashes of insight lit by the blue light our five senses.

If through a tremendous effort, we are able to make out the discernable mosaic through study and great effort, the revealed mosaic is the truth, but in code. The key to that code is a transmitter that exists in that place where there are no words. Someday, maybe wordlessly, we will know the truth. For now, it was enough to know that my daughter's life had mattered, that mine still mattered. I sat on a high promontory overlooking a site of His creation and I let that emotion pour back in once again. Then I went back a year in time and was back on the rock waiting for the boat to return.

Hours later, the charter boat did return. It had picked up the couple upriver from me first, and they were in the boat also, along with a slew of fish. After I got in the boat, the charter boat guy asked me about the net. I told him I had lost it when I fell in the river. He had glanced at the couple and said nothing. Later, on the way back to O'Brien Creek, he asked me if I fell "all the way in." The two of us were sitting in the back of the boat next to the roaring engine. The other couple was out of earshot. I just nodded. He looked at me real funny then and said, "Don't worry about the net." He didn't look at me for the rest of the trip.

Becky was waiting at the boat launch. She was frantic. She came rushing up to me and said, "I'm so mad at you! You almost died, didn't you?" I was speechless. "Didn't you? You almost drowned, didn't you?" The operator of the charter boat just stood staring, unbelieving. Once again I asked him about the lost net. He just shook his head and walked away. Between feeling sorry for me, and disbelief at what Becky had just said, he was happy to just get away. I walked with Becky back to the motorhome. She later told me that she had had a terrible feeling of dread. For the last four hours she had been waiting for the boat to return. I just shook my head. When I told her, she broke down. She wouldn't let go of me. A year later, I sat on the tailgate of my truck and looked downriver trying to find the spot. But that spot was gone. It would live as a memory, I expect forever, but the spot itself was gone. Not surprising. All it takes is a little rain, or not enough rain and the river is changed. It is never the same for very long. So, I have been misleading you all along. Much as I had been misleading myself for years. My supposed search for my spirituality kind of took the same course for me. It started that day, but had I been paying attention, it ended that day as well. Even the seagulls had their priorities. It had just taken me awhile to discover mine. That's what it's all about -- priorities.

What of spirituality? What of knowledge? I choose to believe that knowledge exists where you are able to find it. I should think the same holds true for spirituality. Let's look to another book.

In a book called *The Poisonwood Bible,* a missionary family is set down in pagan Africa in the 1960's. A very dogmatic Baptist minister and his family are battling the elements and ignorance to bring Christianity to the pagans. The family consists of four girls and their mother, along with the strict, fundamentalist father. The girls are struggling to reconcile all they see and hear with the strict scripture of their father. So in the midst of all this, a Catholic priest shows up with his own brand of spiritualism. And he says, "When I want to take God at his word exactly, I take a peep out the window at His Creation. Because that, darling, He makes fresh for us every day, without all the dubious middle managers." The middle managers being all the various versions of the Bible and those who administer it to us. Same thing as Romans 1:20.

The river toyed with my mortality that day. The work of God? It was certainly the work of the River, His creation. Mere chance? Who knows and does it matter? Science can send men to the moon, but not one scientist can explain God. Physicists are plumbing sub-atomic particles only to find that they aren't particles at all, but energy, so-called string theory. Vibrating strings. Pure energy. God, maybe. I'm of the opinion that by the time these scientists plumb the true nature of God, it will change like the River. Some things are not meant to be known. The frontiers of science keep moving ahead, just like they say the Universe is continually expanding at about the same pace as they are catching up -- a treadmill. You gotta have faith baby. You find your faith at exactly the same place you find your truths. The Black Witch would live with me always. That was a truth I got from my friend Paul. He had lost a child also. He said you never get over it. You just live with it. You just live with the Black witch. It's not a part of life you enjoy, but I suppose cancer is that way. You don't enjoy it, but you win or you lose on any given day and hold out hope for tomorrow.

Six months after I left that river that day I went on a snow machine ride across part of Alaska in the wintertime. I guess that ride was kind of a test for the new man that I had patched together after a couple of years with the Black Witch. That ride across Alaska was one of the highlights of my life. It was also a time when I was left to consider some of the events that had altered my life in a negative way. It turned out that it would take two years to retrieve my crashed airplane. After the first year I was on my way home, still thinking about the trip and about other things that had plagued me so.

I had come a long way in those last two weeks. I had driven across a good part of Alaska. I had snow-machined an area larger than some states. That ride had been kind of a settling pool for my thoughts. I had let some of those thoughts drop to the bottom of that pool to make sediment there. That residue was better left to form around the fossils of dead-end thinking. The pool I now swam in was filled with thoughts for further consideration. One of the most important I think, was what Jim Morrison called being "out here on the perimeter." The very edge of experience. Driven there by religion, science or drugs maybe. Some people are obsessed with finding answers to ultimate questions to the point that all other considerations are subordinate to their obsession. To what end? That answer was maybe best elucidated by none other than Albert Einstein. "Man tries to make for himself in the fashion that best suits him a simplified and intelligible picture of the world. He then tries to some extent to substitute this cosmos of his for the world of experience, and thus to overcome it.... He makes this cosmos and its construction the pivot of his emotional life in order to find in this way the peace and serenity which he cannot find in the narrow whirlpool of personal experience. .... The supreme task... is to arrive at those universal elementary laws from which the cosmos can be built up by pure deduction. There is no logical path to these laws: only intuition, resting on sympathetic understanding of experience, can reach them...." This passage was from a speech made by Einstein in 1918. I read these words in Mr. Pirsig's book. The trouble is, I am no Jim Morrison and certainly no Einstein, though after a rough night, some people say I look like him. The point being, that it is best left for people like Morrison to live on the perimeter, and for people like Einstein to tackle the supreme task.

Here is that word again, "esoteric." There are those of the human race, the esoteric few who are driven to understand how the Universe works, the quarks and the string theory. There are those who seem closer to God, the Moses's of our time. I wouldn't begin to guess who our Moses's are these days, but they must exist. The proliferation of prime time evangelism may keep them obliterated from our view. But there are people of science and religion and business and art, etc., who are born with special talents, insights understood by just those esoteric few. At an early age these talented few are then obsessed to focus on the object of their talent, and those few have the incisive intellect, talent and drive to further man's knowledge. Those few have the ability to peer into the storm of mysteries and remove a cloud or two from God's thunderstorm and maybe just glimpse the eye. The rest of us are merely groping. I speak only for myself, though I know there are multitudes like me, people who think that they have the elevated intelligence to grasp some of these secrets, but who are really just trodding on a mental landscape rife with land mines. I think that my inadequacies are inherent in me for a reason. You must contribute as you can, leave the apparition of your own inflated significance behind, see the image in the mirror as it stares back at you and leave the fanciful illusions in the wastebasket beside the toilet.

The simple fact is, the elemental questions of life are best left to those who are equipped to inquire into those questions. It is the duty of these gifted few to assimilate their gleanings and distill them in such a way that the rest of us can begin to understand. To the common man, whom nobody admits to being, except maybe me and my brother Tunda, but who, by definition, encompasses most of us, must find his or her peace on earth. Their reward may lie in the hereafter, but their peace lies on earth. Some of our leaders and most of the media confuse pacification with peace. There can be no other explanation to the garbage they spew.

What is the secret to finding this peace? I hope the reader is not tiring of me quoting other people, but when I see something that sparks my soul, I like to pass it on. Again I go to Whitman: "Dismiss whatever insults your soul" and to Antoine de Saint Exupery: "It is only when we become conscious of our part in life, however modest, that we shall be happy. Only then will we be able to live in peace and die in peace, for only this lends meaning to life."

At one time, I had tried to be a person I simply was not. I lost ten years of my life. I wasted time that would have been better spent knowing my kids. Later, I tried to recreate my past. Stupid and costly mistake. Nostalgia is OK; trying to resurrect ghosts is like starting at the last falling domino and working backwards. So do the best you can and remember those things of which you are proud. Try to recreate the juices that spawned those times.

I remember once when I was flying in my airplane. It was a beautiful fall day. I was out just looking around and I had just over flown the sandbar, "drug it" to make sure it was clear. Dan and Harvey, two Hercules captains that I worked with, were standing at the wrong end, the direction I always avoided landing when I could. Not on this day. It was dead calm. I circled to land, knowing that they were there watching. It was that time in my life when I was most proficient in my airplane. I set up and put it exactly where I wanted it, right on the first two feet of the sandbar, touched down in a wheel landing and held the tail wheel up until just before too much speed bled away, then eased the tail down as soft as momma's kiss. Yeah baby, that was so sweet. That was the beginning of the end to what should have been just the beginning for me. I stopped, turned aside and never looked back until it was much too late, and for ten years that same airplane lay crippled on that same sand bar.

The image of that day, landing the airplane, brought me then back to the snow machine trip to rescue that airplane. Maybe that trip, that snow machine trip to recover that airplane, was the first step in changing all that. Or maybe the trip was the thing itself. I could never rescue my former self, but I could rescue that airplane. And I could begin to put myself back in the seat of that airplane and see what my present self could do with that. The past was frozen into the history of the last century. But the spirit that had lived then, my spirit, was not yet frozen. If I could put that spirit back in shape, revitalize that man who was always eager for a new day, the man who was confident, the man who was gaining skill in something that held passion for him. That man who was unbowed. Scars were a fact of life now and would be so until the time I finally retired. The day that first shovel full of dirt rattled onto my coffin. Maybe the trip to rescue my airplane had finally brought me back to who I was. I was with people who I liked and respected. Maybe religion is a false trail. Maybe the answer was simply to cast off the lamination of fifteen years of failure. Slide out from under that dead weight and leave it behind. Accept the fact that I am a simple man, a common man with simple needs. Get back to the core person.

In order to get back to the core person, I had to face my personal failures. Western culture, no, American culture, is full of labels. Successful is one. Failure is one. Beautiful is one. Mainstream is one. Alternative is one. There are whole regiments of people in this country that march to the tune of material wealth. The reason is that success and wealth are so closely related in this country as to appear as identical twins, almost. But no mother of identical twins could ever mistake one child for the other. Each is so different from the other, that they are unmistakably different. Society at large however, knows no difference between the two.

Ninety-nine point nine per cent of all the people in America want to be rich. Me included. But truly, success lies wholly in your mind; money lies holy, in a bank. A person's success is the most closely guarded secret in any life. All people look for success, most say they have found it, but how many achieve it? How many actually achieve personal wealth, self-respect, self-esteem, requited love, fulfilled accomplishment and of course their own personal version of spirituality? No idea. I only know about me.

Failure is the inverse of success. Only you know, deep in your heart, if you are a failure. Other people simply speculate. The most prominent scientist of the twentieth century may have been a failure. The single greatest conceptual leap in the scientific community since Isaac Newton was the formulation of the theory of relativity. This startling insight achieved at a relatively young age, launched Albert Einstein, like a rocket, onto the pinnacle of physics. He is equated with genius. His famous equation is recognized universally. Yet, perhaps in his own mind, he was a failure. After his greatest discovery, if a leap of conceptional insight can be called a discovery, he spent the remainder of his life trying to reconcile his theory of general relativity with the other great body of theoretical physics, quantum mechanics. He failed. For thirty years he failed. Maybe it was the Job-like determination and the reverence he held for physics and his ultimate failure to tame it that bade him to state somewhat whimsically, "We have to do the best we can, it is our sacred responsibility." Einstein failed in his quest of the Unified theory, as he called it. If the namesake for genius can fail, I guess the rest of us are allowed to also. With the qualification, stated by that genius, you do the best you can.

Everyone is in search of the truth. What is the truth? Antoine de Saint Exupery said, "Truth is not that which is demonstrable, but that which is ineluctable." You will know the truth, when you cannot escape it. I know the truth. The truth is that there are 365 days in the year, more or less. Five to ten of those days I will begin with a malevolent force seated firmly on my chest, pinning me down. I call that force the Black Witch. She first pinned me down on a bed in Wrangell. She took a pair of rusty, serrated scissors, then with knee on my chest, she cut out a piece of my heart, dangled that piece in front of my eyes and with divine purpose, walked to the toilet and flushed that piece of my heart down the toilet. The day my daughter died was the day the Black Witch was empowered with those scissors, and as she will, she chose her spot to use them.

"Helpless" is one of those meaningless words that can scorch your soul. On those days, I should not drink, though I probably will. The truth is, that the hole that that witch ripped out of my heart still remains. No amount of faith, spirituality, love or psychoanalysis is going to change that. It will be there if Jesus Christ himself steps into my living room tomorrow to lift me directly to heaven. I will simply go into heaven with a hole in my heart. My friend Paul, sitting in the Boatel one day, told me you never get over it, you just learn to deal with it. That is the Truth. There is simply nothing to be done except live with part of your heart cut out. No amount of whining will change it. No amount of ancient wisdom will change that. No amount of prayer will change that. Jim Morrison was kind of a freak and maybe a drug addict. He was certainly a drunk at the end, but wisdom is where you find it. He said, "You cannot petition the Lord with prayer." And you can't, at least about dead kids. You cannot petition the Lord with prayer about dead kids. That is an empty box.

To anyone who might object to me giving the female gender to this terrible force that resides in me, I have no apologies, but I offer this explanation. I have experienced the depth of feelings that have found form in this thing I call the Black Witch very few times in my life. A depth of emotion that is so profound and so intense that I have no control over it. I am left only to observe and to endure. Every single time, without fail, that I have experienced emotions that compare with this terrible thing inside me, it has in some way been connected to a female. No man has the power to affect my emotions so intensely. Hence, she, this force, will forever be, to me, The Black Witch.

There are a few people who, while in this mortal world, are forced to run a gauntlet. They alone know about that esoteric gauntlet that they are forced to run. You can take this football and run that gauntlet off in any direction, and there will be a crowd there to cheer you on. But by the very nature of this situation, it is a personal journey. Esoteric, known to few. The few who travel this road must make their own absolutions. A cheering crowd is nothing more than distraction. Well-meaning platitudes offered as either wisdom or scraps of solace fall on deaf ears. Unless you run that gauntlet, you are simply the noise of the crowd. The fact remains that if you know about that gauntlet, then you know it is a hole, or it is a window that opens to the future. If you truly know what that gauntlet is, then you possess the knowledge of the ages, you know the truth. Of this truth, I know nothing.

I do know some truths. The truth is, that I am my father's son. Every time I raise a drink to my lips, I run the risk of letting loose his spirit. Most times this is a good thing. He likes to laugh, he likes to tell stories, he likes to dance. Sometimes though, when the metaphysical moon is full, when the Black Witch is crouching in the corner of my mind where the chains to dark man are secured, crouching there, cackling there, she'll begin to laugh and unsnap those chains, let him loose, release dark man. Dark man is that part of my heritage where the uncivilized European barbarian still offers homage to a full moon. Basking in the shafts of that brooding moon, dark man will begin his decadent dance, sometimes leading, sometimes following the Black Witch. That dance, that dark dance, is the one thing that may be my undoing. Quit drinking? I suppose that would be prudent. Would that root out dark man, or just keep him locked up and brooding? Should you keep dark man locked up, brooding and scheming, or let him dance once in a while? What harm in killing him altogether, somehow? How? When you start killing those things that are part of you, is there a line that you come to that says enough? Is that line drawn by the warden of your spirits or the spirit of Jesus? Or your wife? Your psychiatrist maybe? The mores of this new century? Maybe dark man is simply a pressure valve who needs release once in a while. I think that dark man is a puppet of the Black Witch. I think a snow machine ride over an expanse of purity, bullshit strewn generously around a wood-heated cabin and the shining face of a blond haired wonder, will in time drive stakes into dark man, pin him to a wall in some chamber in my head. There, under the unremitting light of new days, I can cut and examine, cut and examine. I can, at my own pace, cut out the vital parts of dark man's soul, cut him to the point that he falls into a heap at the feet of the Black Witch. With no dance partner, that Black Witch will have to turn her attention to me. And me to her. Her alone, me alone.

The truth is, that any time I look into the eyes of a friend like Jim Wilde, any untruths or bullshit I choose to utter will be lit up in neon, his reaction of shaking head, one more nail in the coffin of my credibility. The truth is, that on those days that I wake up, reach over and touch that beautiful spirit that is my wife, that day, I have an antidote to any dark forces.

I know the truth is in the eyes that stare back from the mirror every morning and not in any words that spew from the mouth of people along the way. The truth is in the light that shines from the eyes of tiny babies. Truth is in the sweat of your palms when you are fixing to land in a twenty-knot crosswind. The real truth lies in that warden who rules your mental prison. You hope he gets his orders from the Good Book. But most of all, the truth lies in the mountains that rise in a ring behind the village of Tanana, the truth lies in the huge trees that are a mile's walk from a place called Wilsonina and the truth runs endlessly in the turgid brown waters of the Copper River.

The truth? Well the truth is that snowflake thing again, for people like me. The universal truth? I believe that it exists. Those who possess a genius level spirituality, maybe they know the truth. People who make the Leap, the leap of faith, what of them, those people who are the body of Jesus? If their personal universe welds them with like souls in that immaculate body, then I guess it swings both ways, this body of Christ. If your personal universe is one and the same with the universal truth, than you are saved. People who know any sort of universal truth dwell in the clouds, at genius level or they were able to make the Leap. But even those who know of those truths, cannot impart them to us common folk, not literally at least. Any universal truth is a divine thing, it's unapproachable except to those with genius and those who have made the Leap, and they cannot literally tell us. So what is their job?

I guess the job of the Leapers is to cajole and live by example. The job of the genius is to take those truths, those universal truths, and fabricate an icon. Take that icon and breathe their spirituality into it. The soul has to be the crucible of our spirituality. It can be nothing else, but more, it has to be the fountain as well. So Mozart took his truth and turned it into something we could hear. Van Gogh took his spirituality and turned it into something we could see. Michelangelo, something we could see and touch. Just a glimpse. Just a fleeting, furtive thing, just the smell of a Sonja rose on a bright spring day, the magenta-colored birch lining the far away flanks of a ridgeline, viewed from a promontory on a spring day so bright and clear as to hurt your eyes. The most the geniuses of the world can hope to impart is just a glimpse of any universal truth. So you are left to discover your personal truths, guided by the soul that is your personal divinity. Proverb 8:36: "He that sinneth against me wrongeth his own soul: all they that hate me love death."

The Good Book. My pursuit of becoming a part of the body of Christ ended finally for me on a frozen plain, staring up at a hand-written sign. I read the Bible twice cover-to-cover, am now about half way through again. Understanding fully the words in that divine tome, is to me like understanding absolutely the entire works of Shakespeare. It is like finding unequivocally your perfect place in nature. It is simply giving yourself, in an immaculate sense, totally to another being so He can do with you as He pleases. Any cheating on this commitment brings the worst kind of punishment. Any of these things require a total commitment, at least in my view. Thoreau believed that to understand any Greek philosopher, you had to read them in Latin, period. How many translations has the original text that now is the Bible, gone through? How many languages?

I found in that book of long ago, Mr. Parsing's book, the idea that works for me. I approach the Christian religion as a pathway to spiritual wisdom and as a solid set of social values. I am not, by definition, one with Christ. I do not know if I will ever be. The rules to get in are too stringent, the penalties for deception, unremitting and harsh. The Rapture requires that you abandon all sense of rational thought and give yourself up to blind faith. It is a requirement. I will never understand Shakespeare, nor will I ever read the great philosophers in Latin. I never expect to extract the wisdom of the Bible. Having said that, In a Christian sense, my fate must be sealed. So why go to church or why read the Bible? I can only say that those people who are the body of Christ, whatever their stated secular position, are the last hope. The proposition that you must love your neighbor is the last hope of mankind. If you apply that principle in all its broad implications, there is hope. Without that principle we are doomed. God is love, and love is our last hope.

An incredible thing happened when I was doing the final rewrite to this book. I went to a used bookstore in Anchorage, one I had never ever seen, let alone been to before. In it I found a slim volume with faded and browning pages. Some of those pages fell out, when later, I was reading that book. The book is called *The Inhabited Universe*. I was surprised to find out that the author had come to some conclusions about God that were startlingly similar to my own. In that book, I found a passage that best elicits my idea of God, and surprisingly, that passage is a quote of Albert Einstein. "My religion consists of a humble admiration of the illimitable superior spirit who reveals himself in the slight details we are able to perceive with our frail and feeble minds. That deeply emotional conviction of the presence of a superior reasoning power, which is revealed in the incomprehensible universe, forms my idea of God."

At some point in my search for spirituality, I had to confront the Book. I have a friend in Jesus, I also have a friend in Spinoza and Pirsig. As in all things, I think if you are honest you must face the truth. And the truth is that which does not insult your soul, and from which you cannot escape. For if you are spiritual, the first thing you must acknowledge is the fact that you are somehow in some way divine in nature. You have a connection with things eternal. But if your mind blocks off traditional ideas, then you must find some mental refuge that can accommodate the history as written in Scripture. Or you must abandon that text. But so much of the New Testament is documentable. Not all of it, but enough so that it presents an implacable dilemma for a practical mind. That, and there are just too many intelligent people who are captured in the truth of those words. Logic becomes a moribund barricade standing in the path of an advancing army of pragmatic *and* enchanted Christian soldiers. It's like wading through an endless airport of Hare Krishnas who are all armed with PhD's in pandering and you only have a Bachelor's degree in philanthropy. Your resolve finally breaks down in the endless assault of a superior dogma and you are left to abandon your logic entirely, rationalize your charity, or finally examine the faith that produces so many tithe mongers. But if God is real, as laid down by Scripture, then you must make some logical sense of it all. So you walk out on the thin ice. The only question is, does the truth lie in the thin layer of logic that keeps you out of the water, or in the water itself? Being an Alaskan, I prefer the ice to the cold water.

I go to my friend Spinoza who is pretty much in line with Pirsig on the issue of Moses. Spinoza was from a Jewish Portuguese family whose ancestors got caught up in the Spanish Inquisition. Forced to convert to the Catholic faith, his ancestors probably accepted their new religion in name only. Sometime in the first decade of the seventeenth century, Spinoza's family fled to Amsterdam to escape a religion that had been forced upon them. But now, centuries of Catholic indoctrination was not easily shed. In those days in Portugal, if you attended university, then it was a Catholic university. So your education was also laced with theology. Spinoza's family was one of many who had fled Portugal to Amsterdam. The educated of those families had been immersed in Catholic doctrine and now reconverted to the Jewish faith of their ancestors. So the Jewish community where Spinoza was raised had a religious identity crisis during his formative years. Spinoza's first studies were focused on the Talmud, the Hebrew language and the Bible. But now, he was living in a city of culture and diversity. His natural curiosity led him to study Latin, which led him to some of the classic Greek philosophers. We can infer from his longevity in philosophical circles that he was gifted. So now, a gifted Jew with a Catholic background, steeped in the wisdom of ancient Greece scratched his head and a radical was born. My kind of guy. They soon kicked him out of the Jewish church. He turned his back on the strict dogma of the Jewish faith, left Amsterdam for the country, and started thinking on his own. It is said he died in serenity, well cognizant when his final days approached. He seemed to live what he spoke. "A free man thinks of nothing less than of death, and his wisdom in not a meditation upon death but upon life." Bring it on God, I spent my life figuring you out and in so doing, I had a good time. I expect that to continue.... forever.

A radical. So when he examined Genesis, the first book of Moses, what do you think he found? He, by now, has read the story in at least two different languages. And here we go again. Me a hillbilly, trying to interpret a book written by a genius, in Latin, translated by a disciple of his, no doubt. The gist of it as I understand it, is that Genesis is a history of the first man written by Moses, in which Spinoza interprets Moses *intended* meaning. He says that Moses said that God was the cause of man's existence. He created man for man's sake alone. Made him free so he could exist in happiness and ignorance. To this end, God forbade man to eat of the tree of knowledge, of good and evil, saying that as soon as he did, man would then fear death instead of desiring life. To help keep man happy, he then gives him a woman. But man ignores God and after he eats the apple of knowledge, he begins to fear death. Spinoza goes on to say that this state of affairs remains until God offers up the spirit of Christ, in Spinoza's mind, the idea of God, and so now death is no longer to be feared.

I don't know that I necessarily agree with all that Spinoza supposed, but what caught my attention was the fact that Spinoza said that this is "what Moses intended" when he was *trying to convey truths*. Moses didn't convey facts -- he *intended* to convey truths.

OK then, if you lend credence to a radical genius of the seventeenth century, then I think that you must try to interpret what Moses said, not read Genesis literally. Same thing that Pirsig maintains and Durant among others. So I think if you want to understand Genesis, then you must put yourself in Moses' shoes. Put yourself in the year 2000 BC. Wipe out all the events that happened after that. Wipe out all ideas of science and technology. Now you must believe fervently in the existence of this great Jewish God. Why? Because he has spoken to you. Whatever really happened, Moses believed in his heart that he had spoken to God.

When Moses trod the earth, how many generations of *intelligent* humans had come before? Where did spirituality come from and when was it implanted? Darwin says that man evolved from prehistoric man. Moses said that God created man. I think they are both right. The mystery is the so-called Missing Link of evolution. And this is where all the fun begins. I think that the missing link is where spirituality was bestowed upon prehistoric man and he was changed into a thinking, spiritual man. The apple of the Garden of Eden is the vehicle that Moses used to describe this event. What I call the Hillbilly theory.

But back to Moses. God has spoken to Moses. How is that possible? Let's say that Moses is twenty generations removed from the Missing Link, the first spiritual man. If Spinoza is right, then God is the sum of all mind. I qualify that; I think God is the sum of all spiritually aware mind, excluding prehistoric man and animals. So if spiritually intelligent mind is the sum of God, then in Moses' time the men possessing that mind were fewer in number than today, far fewer. So what is the bridge between prehistoric man and those that not only stood upright, but walked away with a plan? The missing link is the key to spirituality and to God. The missing link is the progenitor of Moses.

During the time before Moses, men were consumed with just getting by and crashing around like a bull in a china shop just learning to use their newfound intelligence. Along comes Moses, the first true genius. God's matrix, his human pool of spirituality, is relatively small. Suddenly a genius appears -- Moses, who intuitively knows what God is. And since he is among such a small pool of mortal spirituality, and his intelligence is unfiltered and not swayed by any technology, what he has is a main line to the essence of God with no means to explain it. Newton when the apple fell on his head. Einstein when he first scribbled E=mc2. Bam! A flash of insight so intense and so pure that it tingled his toes and he had no one to share it with. But Moses knew. But how to explain it to the morons? And maybe since he was so close to the event and his lineage so pure, he could go back Shirley McClain-style, to the actual event and even know it.

So what did Moses do? Of a sudden we find this genius, whose head is filled with knowledge so fantastic and so intense and so revolutionary.… He was bowled over by his visions, his knowledge and completely helpless to explain it. Newton with his apple, Einstein with his theories. And Moses is overwhelmed with the need to express it, to tell someone, but he can't. What he doesn't know, what he can't know is that his knowledge is just the tip of an iceberg. Like Einstein and Newton, Moses was after all, just a man.

I think when he wrote Genesis, he was writing a children's storybook. The book of Genesis is not a textbook, it is at best, a code book. He wrote a book, Dick and Jane style, for those just learning their spirituality. And because the technology and the science that would explain what he knew were still six thousand years into the future, he resorted to imagery. Thus the great visions, angels and other miracles were created in God's mortal medium, the ability of the human mind to imagine. Our reality is really only two or more people agreeing on terms. What goes on inside a person's head is his alone. His vision, his miracle. His and God's. Wouldn't it be fascinating to inhabit the mind of another person for an hour, just to see what a rose looks like to him?

But back to the vision and the miracles of the Old and New Testaments. Once a witness to a miracle writes down the account of that miracle, the naysayers can then be scoured away by the sands of time. But the event itself -- the miracle? It really did happen in the various prophets' heads. It was real and it was written down, either in textbook fashion if the words existed, or in imagery if they did not. The first few chapters of Ezekiel certainly come to mind.

So was the apple a real apple delivered by some guy in a space ship, or was it imagery for a microscopic bacteria that fell from space, rained down by God, infecting the fruit of that apple? That bacterium, a complex set of amino acids that formed the exact formation of DNA that caused the first scintillating spark of real intelligence to finally deify the hydrogen atom? A set of amino acids whose formation was dictated by God's law, his mandate, physics, nature. Not some random event. Moses told us children, us morons, all about it, if we can only just figure it out. But I truly believe that an event of some sort of divine intervention separates us from simians. I believe that Christianity best illuminates the fact and that we all intuitively feel it and after Jesus appeared to ease our fear of death, most of the other religions of that day were left behind as Jesus and his revolution left many other religions lacking credence and relevance.

I think that we are traveling in a vast circle through space and we will learn the truth about the same time we get back to creation. Heaven? As time has run along a certain portion of its elliptical path, we have arrived at our present. The assimilated souls of the millennia have so enlarged the spiritual pool of God's matrix, that modern day spirituality is much more mundane than in Moses' time, though hardly less significant. In eternity, we all count the same. Moses was far nearer the beginning of the cycle than we are, further down the track. Thus his spirituality and those of his contemporaries were subject to much greater intensity, as they were more one-on-one, so to speak. But everybody has a role and each is as significant as any other. The next true spiritual genius you meet will be Jesus. No one now living will ever be as close to God as was Moses in mortality. But I suppose it is possible for the best of humanity to equal him, in eternity.

I am of the opinion that God is not man-like in appearance or essence. I believe that he is the driving force of nature. I believe that He is bound by laws, not of physics, but of cosmic truths. I believe that good and evil do exist, but must exist, as human events are chained to those same cosmic truths. I believe that it is the nature of divinity that all things are created for a purpose. I believe that the drama we are part of is no drama at all; merely the performance of God's will, the cosmic mandate. Just as a ball that rolls off a desk is mandated to drop to the floor, slave to that force we call gravity, so too are we bound to be born and bound to die. It is necessary. What free will we have and why, is more the mystery.

Since time began, human time, untold multitudes of people have lived and they have all died. Every single one, with the possible exception of Jesus Christ. Why do some people kill and maim and love and hate and spend every waking moment is the pursuit of riches when the whole thing is so futile? Because it is necessary. We have been programmed genetically to be this way. Some gene somewhere demands it. That gene was planted there, and so we must perform like some programmed robot. A slave to a gene planted in the single-celled seed of our zygote. But somehow, some way, the hydrogen atom we share with the sun is part of it all. A thread we share with the sun and with God is also planted in that single cell. That thing is eternity, it is God and it is the seed to our will, or more accurately, the requirement of this seed, this soul, that our will be forged in such a way as to both drive the Cosmic nature of God, yet stamp it somehow, with our infinitesimal, yet significant imprint. Even though we possess this will, we are still slave to the lusts of mortality, and mortality itself. And it is all necessary.

Our lives, in a sense, are like the lives of the dinosaurs. It is said that the decaying flora and fauna of the dinosaur age are one source of the oil we now burn as fuel. The dinosaurs lived and gave up their lives to promote a future civilization. Our lives, in a cosmic sense are the same. We are given a soul so we can contribute. We are given thought as much for entertainment as anything, but along with entertainment of our mortal lives, we are asked to contribute.

I think God is driving a train along a track laid out by his own cosmic mandates. This is another Pirsig analogy. There can be only one destination, because there is only one track. The hydrogen atom is a single electron spinning around a single proton. The electron is slave to that orbit and the hydrogen atom is the most basic building block in the universe. The earth is the third planet that spins around our sun, which is composed of mostly hydrogen. The earth is slave to its orbit. Our bodies are ninety-some percent water, of which hydrogen is a vital element. We are all slave to our particular orbit.

I think it is God's job to refine the train that runs on the track of His orbit. Make it the best vehicle he can before it gets to the station. But one way or another, the train is going to arrive at the station. Our part in all of this is to help refine the train. Because when God gets to the station, that is only one stop on an infinite journey. He wants the best train he can get for the next stage of his timeless journey.

If we have any purpose in all of this, it can only be to help improve the train. What that takes is not for us to know. And in the end our lives are pretty meaningless if you believe in the concept of time. Because if Einstein was right, then time is fluid in a sense. If you go fast enough, then you can stop time in a relative way. The people lucky enough to be traveling on a train going 186,000 miles an hour are living, relative to the people at the station, forever. But as all things are relative, in their small universe of the inside of the train, those people are aging normally. What this means to me is that while our lives are so significant and so important in the small vehicle of our reality, in essence our lives are as important to the cosmos as the lives of the four or five billion people who have passed before us, are to us. So you can choose to build your mansion, or your fortune, it will all crumble in time.

What is eternal? Only the spark of divinity planted in our zygote, the soul. What of this soul? I think the soul is a paintbrush to paint the train, or a ball bearing to make it run smoother. I think that the Omnipotence of God is a prison also. He is bound by his cosmic mandate, his orbit, the track His train runs on, even if he is responsible for that track and that train. So He must improve the vehicle that propels this mandate to its destiny. So spread out through time and space are the receptacles for his intelligence-gathering. Because even though the universe is God's mandate, still it is eternal and He must learn as well. The number of receptacles is infinite. Each of us, by grace of our soul, is one such receptacle. But the receptacle is a transmitter also. "The fitful flash of an eternal light" as Spinoza calls it. The "soul," as I call it. I don't think that we are all the body of Christ, I think each and every one of us is His portal to the current reality. He is gathering intelligence as He travels on an elliptical track picking up speed via the small bits of intelligence He is able to gather, spinning faster and faster until that hydrogen fuses and He bursts into that Heavenly Rapture that will define Eternity for us all.

I think that God is bound by his destiny. But in order to perfect the transport vehicle to that destiny and maybe to beautify it, He has given us the gift of thought and the power of the soul. Within the brief flash of time given us, we are asked to contribute as best we can. We are asked to beautify and refine God's will, His dream, His destiny. When we die and our bodies are committed to the great carbon pool of mother earth, the only thing that will mark our passing is to contribute as best we can to the beautification of His Dream. So if we have done our best, maybe when our bodies join those of the dinosaurs, maybe that spark of divinity, our souls will be a minute part of the great congealing process that defines the mind of God and we too will become eternal. Our lives and bodies meaningless, left to be consumed by the flame of a later, greater civilization.

And I think that God has a great sense of humor. I think that those of you who make the great transition from mortal souls to become part of the fusion of God's mind, will laugh at your preconceptions. The Great Creator ain't gonna look like some patriarch with gray beard and blue eyes. I don't think he's gonna have a body at all. He is probably invisible, with an intelligence that is ether-like almost, just on the precipice of condensation, captured in a great reservoir of no dimension and no shape. A vast sea of intelligence that floats like a mist through the cosmos, clouding up and raining intelligent life down on some fertile planet once in a while.

But for we mortals in the here and now, I think that we take ourselves and our religion way to seriously. People fight over faiths and sects and interpretations as if they can somehow influence the hereafter by earthly endeavor. I don't think you can change that which is written in stone. You can only adorn it.

Given the nature of time, I think that today is the dynamic narrative. We can change an adjective maybe, or a noun, but never the subject of a sentence. Tomorrow is the next paragraph printed on a page unturned. The whole thing is the narrative. The narrative is not only necessary, but it is the law of God and the basics of physics. Our best scientists have only deciphered the first page of the lengthy tome of the laws of God that are the science of physics. We know the mind of God only in so far as we understand the whole of science. Those of us who are spiritual in nature, and genius in that nature, understand on an entirely different plane those same truths, but still only at the elementary level.

The nature of God and Science are the truth. That truth has been established on the tenets of time. Time may be fluid, but it is set on the same elliptical rail that enslaves electrons, planets, solar systems and galaxies. That part of science that is yet unfathomed is the mystery of

God. Maybe only Moses and Einstein have closed on that same mystery to that same point from the opposite direction. But the whole nature of God is the whole nature of science and it is the truth. That truth was established many millennia ago, is unalterable in essence, though somehow dynamically slaved to time.

Time is such a tenuous and ephemeral substance. When regarded in the infinity of the Universe, any one period is inconsequential as well as ill-defined. What our reality is may be just a trick of God. Our reality may already be part of antiquity. Or maybe just a replay. If you give credence to someone like Spinoza, then you are saying that the most intelligent man now alive is but one tiny synapse in the infinite number of synapses throughout the entire spectrum of time. God. In our brain, our lives are real, happening now. But maybe we are just re-taping an event that happened two hundred million centuries ago in cosmic time. Maybe God can play time like a VCR. Just reviewing our lives to see what he can learn. Like everything else in the universe, it appears that light travels an elliptical orbit and if you give it enough room, eventually it will form a circle. If traveling at the speed of light you can alter time, then time too must travel in an arc. It too must form a circle.

For this hillbilly, all this theory is overwhelming. But you just can't leave everything hanging, so as Spencer and the apostle Paul said, by the grace of God I am what I am. I believe that we, us now living, are just the temporarily fluid part of an unalterable essence. Like maybe God fires a laser through the rock of his truth on a never-ending elliptical path. The present is merely the liquid produced from the laser as it cuts through the rock of Truth and eternity. The present solidifies into the past as the laser moves off into the future, liquefying as it goes, the rock solidifying in its wake. Our present reality is only the rock in liquid form before it takes on its final, eternal essence. We are the metamorphic process that changes the sandstone of the past into the marble of the future. God's laser is the present. We cannot change the vital process. We must accept the reality of the event, the inevitability of it and our powerlessness in the face of it. Through our will, we hope that maybe we can become responsible for a cool looking gem of some kind, buried in the infinity of stone.

In the sense that the Universe is said to have been created from a big bang, it is now in the process of expanding from that big bang, a mandate of God and physics. It must be headed to a predestined natural event. Everything has a cause and an effect, an action and reaction, a process of chemistry or physics. Or if you prefer scripture, we are all in the hands of God. Either way you look at it, our fates are ultimately sealed. Since we are all mortal, we really don't have any real power over our lives. Futility or Rapture are your options.

So in my mind, self-important people are fools. They too will give up their bodies to maggots. Transitory contributions of self-important people will crumble. People who contribute will live eternally. Trump's palaces will fall. Hefner's magazine will rot. But Wilbur and Orville's design will live in a flight to a faraway universe someday. Einstein will sit at the helm of that ship. Moses will be the chaplain, Galileo the navigator, Craig Ventor the ship's doctor and Charles Babbage's Engine will run the ship's systems. Me, I would love just to clean up the garbage on that ship. You must remember, even in the most sophisticated society, there is still a way to contribute, even if only as a janitor.

But kind reader, what importance is there in a hillbilly's perception of God? I don't know. And now that I have gotten it down on paper, I don't care. Most of you, if you have gotten this far, have written me off as a wacko. I tend to agree. What makes it worthwhile to at least consider what I have said though is twofold. One, I have been given the gift of thought by God. I have used that gift to expend a lot of thought, years of thought, to come up with my hair-brained conclusions. Most people don't give God much thought. And two, some part of my soul is now embedded in this page. All I can say is God made me do it.

"The words of the prophets are written on the subway wall…." Paul Simon, like my friend Colin, must have met Jesus in an alley. I finally found the words of my prophet on an expanse of tundra in Alaska. The words of my prophet were written on a bleached board nailed to a pygmy black spruce, fifty miles as the crow flies north of the town of Tanana.

It was on the first year of the trip to rescue my airplane from a snowy grave. I was snow machining with the Wilde Bunch, returning from the valley of the Melzoi. Jack was towing my airplane. We had just run over that expanse of a sea of snow named the "Promised Land" by some few residents of Tanana, Alaska. The sign was posted at the entrance to that Promised Land. We had seen the sign on our way to the Melozi, and now, after living the wonderful experience of those few days, I pondered that sign as it again came into view.

I like to think my prophet posted that sign as he was leaving. I like to think that he had driven some dogs into an arctic blizzard. I like to think that after living in the deep cave of an artic night, he found Himself, in an eerie short-lived day. The snow was blowing sideways through the gates of hell to form an hallucination in his path. All landmarks, form itself was bleached out of reality in that perpetual indefiniteness called a whiteout. Not surrendering himself or his dogs, he persevered. Simply refused to give in. And in that place of no substance and no form, he cried out to his God. The response he got saved him and was forever indelibly stamped into his brain in words that he could understand implicitly, being a common man. The storm abated. He continued on across that expanse of frozen forever to its end. When he finally came to a tree, he knew he was saved. And wishing to pass on the truth he had found to others who might pass this way, he left his wisdom, there on that tree. His legacy, his truth, his prophecy, his advice, his soul, the words God had given him in the teeth of a pure white hell. Simple words for a simple man. "No whimpering." And he went on his way. I like to think that is what happened.

I sat that same night, the prophet's sign still as scintillating in my head as the unseen sparks that popped at intervals inside the confines of a barrel stove. It was the last night on what had been a grand adventure for me. We sat around the cabin, me and the Wilde Bunch, Jim, Dave and Jack. The three of them looked like modern day misfits. Born out of time. I found that I had more in common with them than I had with the reality of modern day America. It had to be, it was necessary that I must be a misfit also. And that night I was glad about that. That night I sat in a cabin from the year 1840. Outside sat a machine, a time machine. In the morning I would climb on that time machine, a 1996 Polaris 600 XLT time machine that would transport me back to modern day America in the space of eight hours. And maybe, just maybe, that time machine had taken me back to where I belonged. Along the way it had showed me the sign.

So all my searching, all my drunken rambling, all the advice, everything came to such a simple but elegant summation. "No whimpering." The road to the prophet was traveled with the Wilde Bunch over a frozen land of unmatched splendor. The way had been paved by my brother-in-law Tom, Hopi, Gwen, Stan, Trapper Tom and many others. The only salvation analogy required, sat with broken wings at the end of the trail. I read the words of the prophet on a sign of weathered wood, posted at the entrance to a place called the "Promised Land." It was a real sign and it said, "No whimpering"

Two days after I saw that sign, I was riding south toward my home into a strengthening sun. On other days my thoughts may have been heading south as well. On this day they were not. I thought of some good days. Then, oddly enough, I thought about an obituary I had read recently. It was the most touching thing I had read in some time. It was the short story of a short life. It told the story of a four or five-year-old girl. Yeah, some days I read the obituaries of kids. The mother must have written it, yeah. You could see the bittersweet pain of a mother in those words. This obituary mentioned that her little girl's favorite song was "Harvest Moon" by Neil Young. In my mind it is one of the most poignant things I had ever read. To think of a four-year-old girl sitting and listening to gritty old Neil. You can almost see the hard edges falling away as Old Neil melts into a pool of light in the little girl's eyes. You can then see the mother drowning in that pool as she listens to the same song and imagines that light.

Then I thought about the day that Becky and I had gone to Washington to visit Tasha and Ben. Tasha was about ten I guess. She was as pretty that day as she was the day they took my favorite picture, her at about age two, holding a rose. On this day she sang us the song -- performed it really, "The Rose." That particular memoryscape may be my very last conscious thought when I leave this earth. I expect that from now on, forever, when those first eight single notes on the piano pound like a sledge hammer on my heart strings, then the Divine Miss M softly leads in, the vision will begin again. I will for a period of three minutes be able to imagine her face, hear her voice and remember that ten-year-old girl exactly as she was on that day. That day receding farther and farther into the mists of time. That song evokes a spirit, not a memory, a live spirit. My little dead Tasha lives in that song. If that makes me crazy, then fit me for a straightjacket. For three minutes, every once in a while, my Tasha lives again. Bittersweet is so much better that sad. A different universe really. And now as you read these words, she lives still, here in this book.

What causes you to be flooded by an emotion that covers you like paint? Why can that song lock me into a three-minute prison? A prison of velvet, stained with tears. What word describes a rush of emotion so strong that it feels like you are drenched in adrenalin? Makes you feel so sad and so happy that you have to cry. What does a parent think when they see me looking at their young daughter, a little girl with blonde hair and laughing eyes? A little stranger in a grocery store or sitting in a car next to me. What is that thing over which you have absolutely no control? Is it the opening to the hole of the oblivion, or is it simply a small peek through the window that serves as the portal for the afterlife? The first real opening into that black that exists beyond the limit of years on this planet. What of it? What of the last hope for immortality?

Then I thought of that day in the airplane. It was a day much like this day, only it was September, not March. It was a day in my 27th year. We had landed at Manley on the way back from the Melozi. We had our dead moose. Dan was flying his Cub and I was alone in my C170. We got enough gas in Manley to get us home. And we took off.

When you take off on some days, you simply elevate. When you rise above the detailed world of buildings and runways and trees that are individual plants, the landscape becomes a tapestry. A blending of colors and shapes that are no longer trees or rivers, they become patterns. When I arose above tree-level, the Alaska Range looked like it was five miles away, though I knew it was more than 100 miles. The Sawtooth Mountains were within the reach of long arms. The world was on fire, dying leaves absolutely dazzling. All was captured under a sky that capped the world in a bowl of deep blue. I didn't fly over the land that day, I was captured like an insect in the amber of that blue sky and the landscape just slowly rotated away from me and towards me. No feeling of motion at all, the air was as still as the peace in my heart.

Someone once said that architecture was music, frozen. If that is so, then on that day in that airplane under that sky, that wilderness was frozen music, enslaved music, set free. Pick your favorite song. On that day, it would have been "Something in the way she moves." On that day so long ago, "Something in the way she moves" was set free by the spirit of George Harrison, it was then emulsified and ceded to the spirit of Vincent Van Gogh. With my spirit in mind, the spirit of Ol' Vincent painted the scene, horizon to horizon. Thanks to the spirits of Wilbur and Orville, I was able to see it like no one else ever did or ever will. We were the only ones in the sky that day, me and Dan, and George, and Vincent, and Orville and Wilber. And we were all alone. And that day is frozen. It's frozen in my mind, a gift to me from the spirits.

But as spirits are wont to do when they are free, they show up at will. And now I also knew that the Black Witch controls spirits as well. No matter what my mood, she can and will, pick her spot. And on that day, driving south into the sun, my airplane tethered to a tree at the entrance to a place called the 'Promised Land', she came to me again. And of course she brought me back to the incident. That day in the river. The incident. So, now slave to other spirits, I went back there. I was in the river again. But now let's pretend that the year was 1395, not 1998. Let's pretend I am writing these words for the people of Genoa, Italy in the year 1395.

A lifetime. My lifetime lay in my hands. My mind was split into five equal parts. Each part of my mind was being held hostage by a demon or a spirit. A demon, his red eyes piercing, spoke "I am called Camus, I come from the future, sent here by our father. I am here to take you home to Him." At his side, the evil Black Witch. She, the handmaiden to Lucifer himself. Staring intently, intelligent, scintillating eyes sparking with fire, Camus spoke again. "Do you choose to come home to your father now?" The question was a slap in the face of my manhood and an abomination to the glory of God. But still, I was speechless. My spirit was drunk with the power of its own will to survive. The Black Witch was now in possession of my mind, her greedy hands reached out for my soul. I could smell the stench of her hot breath, the breath of eternal hellfire. An evil thing. She embraced me then, her green hands could I feel, wrapping around the back of my neck. My heart was heavy with the weight of those hands, my will was slipping. I was falling into her trance, her eyes glowing like burning coal, just inches from mine. I was slipping away, being seduced by a great evil. She changed just then, her evil green face melting into that of a vamp, a beautiful siren, singing her eternal dirge, so enticing, so seductive. I felt myself sinking into her trance. I was immersed in the great river. It reached to my eyes, pushing me down towards the depths by the very weight of the demons. Suddenly, the glow of truth burst into my breast. The great son of God, *Jesus, stopped the flow of the river*! I was awestruck by the power of his truth as it cascaded into my soul. The truth, His truth. Now the work of His hands had stayed the flow of the great river. The river of his creation. Now, oh could I only be on my knees! Then the great river was not only stayed, it began to flow backwards! I was being swept by divine hands, back to the shore. The evil hands now gripping my throat, tightened.

The end was near, little hope. But no! God was there with me. I am of the tribes from the far north, near the shore of the Western Sea. The lord God summoned the spirits of my forefathers, my saviors, a Hun and a Viking rumbled to life. They had nothing to say. The spirit of my great grandfather was before me, he with his great sword. His terrible swift sword, guided by the hands of my Lord, was just and sure. The evil Black Witch cried out in mortal agony as her head was cleaved, green mush pouring from it. She slunk into a pile of vile, putrid pus. The spirit of my mother's great grandfather leaped toward the demon Camus. The demon's hair had turned into a writhing mass of vipers. My grandfather's spirit grasped the demon by the vile mass that was the demon's hair, ripping him from my mind, he cast that evil demon into the cleansing waters of God's great river. Together the spirits lifted me onto the firmament and I was saved. The demons perished into the depths of the great river.

One day, one battle. As I lay panting on the banks of the great river, I took a moment to pray and thank our great God for my salvation. I was on my knees and I prayed for forgiveness for my weaknesses. The demon Camus is a dupe of Lucifer, a slave to his ego and his intellect. He is a pure intellectual, sterile of spirituality. The Black Witch is a confederate of the devil Lucifer. My battle with her is eternal. By the grace of God, I will persevere. God, in his wisdom will overshadow the evil and guide my days. His Grace is the Truth, the path and the Way. Those evil things of this world are bound by the corrals of the mind, or slave to Lucifer, their entrance is barred from the heart and the soul.

The New Testament is rife with the stories of Jesus casting out demons, spirits, and devils. Those things were observed and recorded by the Disciples. Using an idea first planted in my mind by Mr. Pirsig's book long ago, and given a similar slant by my Pastor, John Henry, I was able to come to terms with the events of that day. A demon had been planted in my mind by the death of loved ones. That demon had been nurtured by stress and other modern day maladies. That demon then summoned the spirit of a dark genius, Albert Camus and the words that genius embodied. When I found myself in a life-threatening situation, the release of chemicals into my body gave form to now real demons and long dead sprits, which were then summoned into my consciousness. My saviors, two barbaric tribesmen from my long ago past, bludgeoned their way into my consciousness and pushing the Black Witch aside, grasped the dark genius by the dreadlocks of his intelligence and ripped him out of my brain. A demon was cast out that day and swept away by one of the forces of God, the Copper River.

Another malevolent demon, the devil perhaps, remains. She waits.

My journey through the dark recesses of my mind was simply all about grief. I had no experience to compare it with for the depths of its emotions and the lack of any viable means to deal with it. So I suffered and I searched, because on an intellectual level there had to be a means to deal with it. There was none. I simply had to endure it. It took a very long time and resulted in no answers of any sort. The search for an answer that made sense was futile. The same as making some sort of logic out of spirituality. It ain't gonna happen and I have learned to accept that. The *no whimpering* sign I found on the edge of the "promised land" is as close as I will ever get. The joy of my remaining days is simply lessened. But don't whimper, deal with it and move on. There are forces in my head that await another traumatic event. The outcome, should that occur, is unclear. I will take the best effort I have in me to leave this world with some sort of grace and dignity. It is the best that I can hope for.

However, the search for the way out of the darkness was a therapy. It occupied my mind when I desperately needed that. In a way, the whole process of looking into some sort of spirituality and the writing of this book was of tremendous value to me. The entire process along with the love and support of my family, mainly Becky, was the light that led me back home.

Epilogue

MAY, 2002, VALDEZ, ALASKA

We were busy at work creating twin, mile-long rainbows over the slate-green water of Prince William Sound. The company where I work has a contract to provide a portion of the spill response effort, should another oil spill occur in or around the shipping lanes that lead from Valdez to the Gulf of Alaska. We are flying at 140 knots. We have the back door and the ramp of the Hercules opened wide. Fanned out, like a crop duster's spraying apparatus, were two twenty foot booms, angled out behind us. Those booms were dispensing water at a rate of 500 gallons a minute. As the water hits the air, delivered through thirty-some odd nozzles on each boom, it is atomized into a ghostly mist and swirls with the wing-driven vortices of the airplane into two rainbows that stretch out behind us for half a mile or more. We are just 50 feet off the water. The two rainbows are like two indelible promises of God's good will.

The ten-foot by nine-foot opening of the rear of the airplane frames a scenery so spectacular as to defy description. In our ten-mile circuits around this great body of water, we can see three glaciers. Snowcapped mountains give way to an uninterrupted infinity of green spruce that reach from the barren peaks, straight down to the green sea that laps onto black beaches at the feet of those trees. Gray and black clouds are rioting around in the courtroom of a bright blue sky. We are practicing for the next oil spill. In that event, we would be dispensing oil dispersant out of the 5000-gallon tank now sitting in the back of the plane. We all hope we will never be given the chance. It is springtime in Alaska, and it's good to be alive.

On a bright morning in August, 2009, I awoke to music playing softly. The music had no source. And I knew. It faded away soon enough and I arose to face it again. Becky had been in the hospital for most of a week. Becky was very tired and she was weary. I didn't know it at the time, but I had three days left with her. I started calling people. She left us surrounded by people who loved her. I found out in the coming months the extent of her battle. Friends of hers, whom I had occasion to talk to, told me of things that Becky had not the heart or maybe the courage to tell me. Her self-confidence was a very fragile armor. She battled demons I had no concept of during the time she spent with me. She was a brave soldier on a battlefield strewn with unreconciled events from her past. I will miss her eternally. Her battle with the Witch ended in God's hands.

My job as a loadmaster ended soon after. The job I had done for thirty-five years was no longer important. Health insurance no longer was a chain I had to drag around. The shaky relationship I shared with my boss ended when I unhooked that chain.

That Christmas, while visiting my son, the Strawberry Blonde enigma was visiting also. True to form, she came busting into the house in a whirlwind and left soon after in a tempest. As an observer, I marveled at the scene and began to think of what was important. Events of thirty years previous, so important at the time, were like dust settled on a highway, traveled long ago. As I write these final words in 2014, Sherry and I are together again in a way we never were before. We are two road-weary pilgrims facing the end of our times.

One week ago I had an occasion to be in California, staying alone in the house where Becky grew up. In the back yard, lying on a 20-dollar blowup mattress I had bought at Walmart for the occasion, I stared into a blanket of stars. The coyotes were just yards away, or so it sounded. Their howling leant a lonely, searching soundtrack. The sky was lit with fire. The dying heat of the day, a warm embrace. There were shooting stars, satellites and maybe a UFO or two. Beyond the light show, on a mountain named Lone Oak, lay a plaque with the short details of Becky's life enshrined on its granite surface. Immersed in the oak trees surrounding her plaque are the ashes of both her and her father. Her father, Dick, a famous man, shared the spot where I now lie. I can see him still, in his final days, sitting in a chair, staring at his mountain, Lone Oak, where he was raised as a child and saying, "Every man should own his own mountain." Dick shares his mountain with his daughter. I envy him that.